TABLE OF CONTENTS

EXECUTIVE SUMMARY	4
INTRODUCTION	6
Overview of Report	7
CHAPTER 1: Arts Education and Social-Emotional Learning: A Theory of Action	10
Developmental Experiences and Relationships	10
A Theory of Action for Arts Education and the Development of Social-Emotional Competencies	12
Art Practices and Social-Emotional Components	14
Art Education Process	15
Art and Social-Emotional Competencies	16
Cultural Beliefs about Arts Education	18
CHAPTER 2: Exploring Arts Education and Social-Emotional Learning in Practice	22
Self-Management and Self-Discipline	22
Interpersonal and Relationship Skills	27
Self-Expression and Identity	31
Summary	35
CHAPTER 3: Conclusions and Implications	36
Opportunity Is Critical to Development	36
Intentionality Ensures That Opportunities Are Fully Leveraged	37
Lessons for Other Subjects	38
What Research Is Needed	39
Conclusion	39
WORKS CITED	41
ACKNOWLEDGMENTS	46

EXECUTIVE SUMMARY

Social and emotional learning is a topic of increasing focus in the education sector. Though definitions and terminology vary, at its core this trend reflects an increased interest among educators, administrators, parents, and other stakeholders in students' development of individual and interpersonal skills beyond the realm of academic achievement.

Across existing research literature and among arts educators there is widespread belief that artistic disciplines including music, dance, theatre, visual arts, literary arts, and media arts have a positive effect on children's and adolescents' social-emotional development. This project investigates the relationship between arts education and social-emotional learning and develops a theory of action describing the nature of that relationship.

This project consists of two components: a review of literature on this topic and an interview-based fieldwork component with educators, administrators, students, and parents in Chicago Public Schools. Our literature review highlights the strength of the research into arts education and social-emotional learning with regard to focused, qualitative case studies and the gaps with regard to experimental or randomized control trials. Combining this arts-specific research with multidisciplinary literature on child and adolescent development and insights from our fieldwork interviews, we propose a theory of action that describes how arts learning experiences have the potential to promote young people's development of social-emotional competencies.

Our theory of action starts from the premise that each large-scale **art education process** (e.g., taking piano lessons, putting on a theatrical production, or doing a lesson on graffiti) consists of many smaller-scale actions (e.g., practicing a piece for a recital, rehearsing a scene, or choosing statements to express through graffiti). We argue that each of these small-scale actions, or **art practices**, also includes **social-emotional components**. To offer just one example for each, the piano practice could include using breathing and mindfulness to deal with performance anxiety, the theatre rehearsal could include working with other students to accomplish a goal with minimal adult supervision, and thinking about expression in graffiti could prompt students to reflect on the feelings about events going on in their lives. Just as the art practices themselves are the building blocks of long-term **art competencies** (e.g., skill at playing the piano, performing a play, or creating graffiti), the **social-emotional components** are the building blocks of long-term **social-emotional competencies** (e.g., improved emotional self-regulation, responsibility and awareness of peers' emotional states, and confidence in expressing complex ideas stemming from personal thoughts and feelings). Our theory emphasizes that the artistic and social-emotional aspects are always happening simultaneously and that, just as a student can learn good or bad piano habits, she can learn good or bad social-emotional habits. Just as the art practices must be cultivated into long-term art competencies through guidance and instruction, the social-emotional components of these activities must be cultivated into long-term social-emotional competencies.

This report has three sections. The first describes our theory of action in greater detail, emphasizing the developmental effects of arts education. The second section surveys evidence in three areas of social-emotional development: self-management and discipline, interpersonal and relationship skills, and self-expression and identity. It also provides illustrative examples of the theory of action drawn from literature and our fieldwork interviews. The third and final section describes practical implications of this work and suggests areas for further research.[1]

Our conclusions are relevant to both the practitioner and policymaking levels. First, exposure to a range of arts opportunities is crucial in helping students to identify and engage with learning contexts that will fit their own social-emotional needs. Second, arts education has social-emotional effects regardless of instructor intent—and these effects can be either positive or negative. It is crucial for educators to be intentional in the social-emotional contexts they create through their lessons. Third, while we argue that arts education is particularly well-suited to social-emotional development for a variety of reasons, it is by no means unique in this regard. There are lessons that educators in non-arts subjects can draw from the mechanisms whereby arts learning has a positive social-emotional impact on children and adolescents.

Overall, this report emphasizes that arts education settings are sites of great potential. Learning literary or media arts, visual arts, theatre, dance, or music has great intrinsic benefits for young people, as they are exposed to creative humanistic experiences and the potential for rigorous skill development. However, with deliberate planning and awareness, a skilled instructor can shape these lessons into spaces for deep and lasting development of those young people's social and emotional skills and well-being.

ArtReach Chicago at Walsh Elementary School

1 To download an electronic version of this report and to view a technical appendix, please visit: https://ingenuity-inc.org/ArtsEd-SEL-Research
https://consortium.uchicago.edu/publications/arts-education-anc-social-emotional-learning-outcomes-among-k-12-students

INTRODUCTION

I think that arts, in a lot of ways, really lend themselves to expression and independence and voice, which under different terms are all parts of social-emotional learning. And so I think there's a very, very natural sort of relationship with the arts and expression. And developing some of those skills—heart, mind and work, compassion, or kindness—because of the way we teach arts here, it involves a lot of collaboration, a lot of partnership and team building, [as well as] demonstrations of what you know. There's a lot of engagement with other people in order to really understand that what you're doing is correct or that you're working toward a goal.

— Arts educator in the Chicago Public Schools

Schools have long played a critical role in preparing students to be productive members of society in adulthood. Over the past few decades, this role has been largely defined in academic terms—ensuring that students have learned the knowledge and skills they need to be successful in college and career. In this context, the value of arts education in school has most often been framed as an instrument to enhance school engagement and academic learning, either indirectly through connections between an arts education and academic outcomes,[2] or directly through incorporating arts curricula with instruction in other subjects (i.e., arts integration).[3]

At the same time, a growing movement is advocating for the idea that the outcomes we ultimately care about in our children reflect a broader set of concerns related to social-emotional development: Are they good and kind people? Are they contributing members of their families and their communities? Are they able to set goals and pursue their dreams? Are they productive, helpful people in the workplace?

The benefits of broadening our understanding of the developmental outcomes of schooling go beyond the individual to contributing to the larger social fabric. In a country that is both rich in diversity and deeply divided socially and politically, with stark and widening economic inequality, many are calling upon schools to teach empathy, social responsibility, civic engagement, and the skills to communicate with one another across differences.[4] Employers and higher education administrators are also emphasizing the importance of "21st century" or "college- and career-ready" skills such as innovation, collaboration, perseverance, and critical

---

2   Hetland & Winner (2001); Melnick, Witmer, & Strickland (2008), Catterall, Dumais, & Hampden-Thompson (2012).
3   Ludwig, Marklein, & Song (2016); Burnaford, Brown, Doherty, & McLaughlin (2007); Deasy (2002).
4   Borba (2018); Kudo & Hartley (2017); Rivkin (2009); Spencer-Keyse (2018).

thinking in young people for success in the workplace and in college. We are interested here in understanding how arts education can influence the development of this broad set of competencies and attributes that we consider under the umbrella "social and emotional" learning.

In addition to the development of particular competencies as desired *outcomes* of learning, researchers from a range of disciplines have demonstrated that the *process* of student learning is inextricably social and emotional.[5] Learning in the arts is no exception. Whether in school or out of school, in self-directed learning or through peer-to-peer interactions, the arts provide a wide range of opportunities for social-emotional experiences as well as developing social-emotional competencies. Some arts education experiences culminate in a polished product or performance meant to be shared; others emphasize the process of creating art performances or products. Sometimes, arts education is viewed as a means of instilling discipline and tenacity by teaching students the exacting requirements of mastering new ballet positions or learning to play runs on the saxophone while instilling the importance of practice. Arts education is also seen as a vehicle for self-expression, helping students explore aspects of their identity and express emotions that are not encouraged at other times in the school day. And some arts education provides opportunities for collaboration and building social skills, for example through being part of a theatre production or a member of an orchestra.[6]

This report examines the intersection of arts education and social-emotional development. We use the lens of social-emotional learning to examine and articulate how arts education, beyond its intrinsic value, can help young people develop into productive, emotionally healthy, and engaged adults. Arts education has a role to play not only in building artistic skills, but also in building critical competencies and mindsets that can be transferred to other subject areas, and as an important part of the overall development of young people.[7] This report investigates how an education in the arts can help achieve these objectives.

Overview of Report

A primary goal of this project is to propose a theory of action describing the role arts education can play in children's social-emotional development and the mechanisms by which arts education can affect social-emotional competencies. We intend that this theory of action will provide a clearer understanding to support adults in organizing arts education experiences that more intentionally provide opportunities for social-emotional development.

To this end, the focus of our model is on *how* arts education fosters social-emotional development. Though many practitioners feel that arts education has a transformative effect on students' personal development, we examine the evidence base for these claims and work toward a better understanding of the *mechanisms* by which arts education might have an impact. While we believe that art—and consequently an education in the arts—matters for its own sake, the aim of this theory of action is to give adults insights to help them be more intentional in leveraging arts education toward social-emotional development.

To conduct this research, we did an extensive review of research literature and held focus groups and interviews with key participants in the arts education process. We talked to arts teachers, teaching artists, arts administrators, and students and their families, to get a picture of how they conceptualize the role that arts education plays in social-emotional development. We interviewed both arts teachers (arts educators on the staff of a K–12 school who usually have education degrees and/or state certification) and teaching artists (arts educators who are not formal members of a school faculty, but have professional experience in the art form they teach) to ensure that we captured a range of perspectives on approaches to teaching in the arts.

We also took a deep look at the literature on arts education to evaluate the evidence, based on its effects on social-emotional learning, particularly in school and after-school settings. Across the research literature, we found much belief and conjecture that arts education contributes to children's and adolescents' social-emotional development. Like previous reviews of the literature, however, we found few studies that were generalizable or sufficiently rigorous to make strong empirical claims about a direct contribution of the arts to social-emotional outcomes as a matter of course.[8] A large percentage of available studies looking at social-emotional outcomes in arts education were qualitative examinations of a particular art program in a particular setting, drawing from researcher observations and participant interviews. Also common were correlational

---

5 Cantor, Osher, Berg, Steyer, & Rose (2018); Jones & Kahn (2017); Immordino-Yang (2016).
6 As discussed in the box in Chapter 1, arts education creates opportunities for each of the 10 developmental experiences identified in *Foundations for Young Adult Success*.
7 *Foundations for Young Adult Success* (Nagaoka, et al., 2015).
8 Hetland & Winner (2001); Melnick et al. (2008).

studies using self-report surveys in which arts program participants reported higher levels of social-emotional competencies than non-participants. Unfortunately, most of these studies lacked sufficient controls or failed to address concerns with self-selection, and few studies used quasi-experimental methods or randomized control trials that could identify causal effects. Further, almost all studies focused on art programs as the unit of analysis rather than attending to the mechanisms whereby a particular art form or type of artistic practice led to specific social-emotional outcomes. In short, existing studies do not provide evidence that would allow us to draw a reliable line between any particular art practice and a corresponding social-emotional outcome.

That being said, the evidence taken as a whole does suggest that the arts have an important role to play in supporting the social-emotional development of children and youth. We provide examples of studies that connected arts participation to social-emotional outcomes, as well as examples from our fieldwork that made similar connections. Importantly, we draw on earlier reviews of the broad, multidisciplinary literature on child and adolescent development[9] to hypothesize how arts education may well provide a particularly powerful context for young people's social-emotional learning.

We have organized the results of this knowledge collection into a theory of action that describes the role arts education can play in children's social-emotional development and the mechanisms by which arts education can affect social-emotional competencies. **Our primary aim for this theory of action is to illuminate for practitioners how arts education can best foster social-emotional development— and consequently to help practitioners be more thoughtful and intentional in their design of arts curricula.**[10] Though arts education can be a powerful force in supporting students' social-emotional development, a major takeaway from this project is that this does not happen automatically. Even where we saw evidence of arts education having significant effects on social-emotional development, there was much variation in outcomes among participants and across settings. In some circumstances, the effects of arts participation can be negative: Young people may feel deeply exposed or ashamed, or come away convinced that they lack creativity or artistic talent. They may well go through life purposefully avoiding future situations involving visual arts, music, theatre, dance, or other art forms that they associate with these painful feelings. This is not to say that arts instructors should shy away from uncomfortable or challenging content or situations— indeed, providing challenge in a safe space is one of the catalytic opportunities available in arts education. Rather, we hope our theory of action helps practitioners to better understand *how* arts education can contribute to long-term social-emotional outcomes so arts educators act responsibly and effectively to create powerful learning experiences that serve the best interests of their students' long-term development.

We have divided this report into three chapters. In the first chapter, we describe our theory of action and highlight the principles of developmental experiences and developmental relationships that underlie it. The next chapter explores what this theory looks like in practice through three lenses on social-emotional development: self-management and discipline, interpersonal and relationship skills, and self-expression and identity. In the final chapter, we provide implications of the theory of action for practice and suggest areas where further research is needed.

---

9 Farrington et al. (2012); Nagaoka et al. (2015).
10 We also see opportunities for this project to yield other benefits. For example, the theory here can support arts education advocates and others who seek to more clearly express why arts education matters by articulating how arts education can play a role in development and engagement in school. For researchers, we hope this project can lay the foundation for future research on the relationship between arts education and social-emotional development, including ways to expand and deepen the conversation to include more stakeholders.

Changing Worlds and Manierre Elementary School

CHAPTER 1

Arts Education and Social-Emotional Learning: A Theory of Action

Human learning is a deeply, fundamentally social and emotional process. Researchers across a broad range of disciplines (e.g., cognitive, developmental, and social psychology; neurobiology; epigenetics; education; youth development; linguistics; sociology; economics) are coming to consensus about the deep interconnections among cognitive, emotional, and social-relational aspects of human functioning, which together form the bedrock of learning and development.[11] Much recent research demonstrates the interconnected nature of learning: from experimental studies showing the importance of human interaction for early language recognition in infants (a phenomenon that can't be replicated by exposing infants to audio recordings of human voices without a physical human speaker present),[12] to research demonstrating that college students' perceptions of their environments impacts their academic performance,[13] to longitudinal studies that identify a boost to learning that comes from a student of color having a teacher of the same race,[14] to functional magnetic resonance imaging (fMRI) technologies that show real-time connections between emotions and thinking in the human brain. These studies largely support what great arts educators and arts theorists have long intuited: that learning is a social and emotional enterprise.[15] It is within this rich and complex social context of learning that we examine the role of arts education in children's and adolescents' social-emotional development.

An especially useful framework for understanding how arts education can help develop social-emotional competencies comes from a comprehensive report from the University of Chicago Consortium on School Research (UChicago Consortium), *Foundations for Young Adult Success: A Developmental Framework*. Two critical concepts in this report—which was compiled through an expansive review of literature, expert interviews, and several regional and national convenings—are particularly helpful in better understanding how arts education might influence social-emotional development: 1) That the way children and youth develop competencies, beliefs, and behaviors is through *developmental experiences*— opportunities to act in the world and reflect on their experiences; and 2) experiences are most influential in shaping the course of development when they take place within the context of strong, supportive, and sustained *developmental relationships* with important adults and peers.[16]

Developmental Experiences and Relationships

Developmental experiences are opportunities for children and adolescents to gain exposure to and act in the world, and to reflect on their experiences. Social-emotional competencies, like virtually all aspects of human development, depend upon experiential opportunities to bring them forth. As children and youth observe their environments, interact with others, and make sense of their experiences, they build not only their knowledge and skills, but an understanding of themselves, other people, and the wider world. Further, they develop habitual patterns of behavior, thought, and feeling in response to their perceptions and interpretations. This is the natural process of learning and development, both in and out of school. In this way, richer, more frequent, and more varied opportunities for action and reflection support young people's social, emotional, and academic development.

---

11 Cantor et al. (2018); Jones & Kahn (2017); Immordino-Yang (2016).
12 Kuhl (2004).
13 Walton & Cohen (2007, 2011).
14 Dee (2005); Egalite, Kisida, & Winters (2015).
15 Dewey (1954).
16 Nagaoka et al. (2015); Search Institute (2014).

Developmental Experiences: How Arts Education Activities Can Build Social-Emotional Competencies

In this report, we draw on *Foundations for Young Adult Success: A Developmental Framework,* and its concepts of developmental experiences and developmental relationships. Consortium researchers identified 10 developmental experiences that were particularly powerful contributors to youth learning and development, including the development of social-emotional competencies. These 10 developmental experiences include five *action experiences (encountering, tinkering, choosing, practicing,* and *contributing)* and *five reflection experiences (describing, evaluating, connecting, envisioning,* and *integrating).* Evidence from a range of disciplines suggests that the more students have the opportunities to engage in these types of experiences, the more developmentally healthy and successful they will be.

FIGURE A. ACTION AND REFLECTION EXPERIENCES

Applying this developmental framework, we can see that arts education may provide particularly powerful opportunities for social-emotional development. Across a variety of art forms (e.g., music, dance, theatre, visual arts), students have opportunities to *encounter* new roles, materials, and concepts as well as models of expert technique. They are able to *tinker* and experiment with these new roles, materials, and ideas. Art settings usually offer young people many opportunities for *choice* in how they want to participate or express themselves, which materials to work with, how to apply color, or how to approach a scene. Opportunities for *practice* are likewise abundant, whether in practicing a piece of music, rehearsing a play or a set of dance steps, singing scales to warm up vocal cords, or making pencil sketches before embarking on a new painting. Finally, arts education offers young people myriad opportunities to *contribute* to something greater than themselves, including larger collective efforts such as a band concert or theatre production, or to express and contribute their views on important social issues.

In addition to these five action experiences, arts education also provides multiple opportunities for students to engage in reflection experiences and make meaning of their work and their engagement in the artistic process. The reflection experiences that arts education commonly affords include opportunities for young people to *describe* their work or their motivations or processes in creating it, as well as to *evaluate* and critique the work of other artists, including their peers. Likewise, across art forms there are ample opportunities for children and youth to *connect* their own emotions, experiences, or artistic work to the emotions, experiences, or works of others; to *envision* finished products before they are brought into being or to envision themselves as working artists in the future; and to *integrate* their artistic experiences and identities into a larger vision of themselves. These powerful opportunities for reflection enable young people to make meaning of their artistic endeavors in ways that can be transformative and enduring.

The 10 developmental experiences in the Consortium framework, applied here to arts education, were drawn from two large bodies of literature: 1) Studies in neurobiology and epigenetics describing how neural connections are created and neural pathways strengthened in the brain during childhood and adolescence; and 2) Studies across a variety of disciplines (cognitive science, philosophy, education, social psychology) focused on how people learn and make meaning of experience.[A] In this report, particularly through our review of the empirical literature on arts education, we used this framework to guide our investigation of how arts experiences might contribute to the social-emotional development of children and youth.

A Nagaoka et al. (2015).

Strong, supportive, and sustained developmental relationships with important adults and peers are critical to making meaning out of developmental experiences and encouraging "young people to reflect on their experiences and help them to interpret those experiences in ways that expand their sense of themselves and their horizons."[17] All educators are in powerful positions to influence the kinds of experiences that young people have within a learning setting as well as the way they make sense of those experiences as they grow socially and emotionally. How a student perceives any particular learning environment and learning task (e.g., how supportive the environment is, how attuned the teacher is to the student's particular needs, how relevant the task is) influences the way the student chooses to engage in learning activities and the extent to which the student puts forth effort or takes risks.[18] Student effort and engagement, in turn, influence the extent to which students reap the developmental benefits of any given experience.[19]

This suggests that particular competencies (e.g., perseverance, a good work ethic, or an outgoing attitude) are not necessarily something a student has or doesn't have, but rather are potentialities that can be brought forth *in response to an environment*. While a teacher cannot be expected to control all elements of a student's environment—the contexts in which arts education happens include much that is beyond a teacher's control—teachers can play an important role in shaping the response a student has to this environment. A student with a teacher who truly cares about them or a subject that truly captivates them might feel what it is like to be inspired to persevere through difficult work, where another student with the same potential may not be so fortunate to experience relationships or conditions that inspire their best effort.

Without positive developmental experiences and the developmental relationships that help a young person take advantage of them, their potential competencies, abilities, and ways of being might lie dormant, unexpressed and undiscovered. Note that this concept of dormant potential suggested by a growing body of research literature[20] is very different from a pervasive view of students as empty vessels to be filled with knowledge and skills. Rather than young people needing to be "taught" perseverance or empathy, we would instead ask what opportunities a given setting or activity provides to draw forth these social-emotional competencies waiting in potentia. It is with this set of understandings that we consider the role of arts education in social-emotional development.

A Theory of Action for Arts Education and the Development of Social-Emotional Competencies

Developmental experiences and developmental relationships are foundational concepts in understanding how social-emotional learning happens. In this section, we draw on those concepts to present a theory of action that describes how arts education can play a role in the development of social-emotional competencies that enable young people to interact productively with others, build and express a healthy sense of self and community, and work effectively toward their goals.

Too often, there is a kind of "black-box" thinking about the connection between arts education and social-emotional learning that obscures, rather than sheds light on, how arts education can influence these outcomes. Arts education experiences are frequently described in ways that suggest they have certain ineffable qualities that magically produce social-emotional learning in young people. One of our goals in presenting this theory of action is to crack open this black box. The theory is intentionally very flexible; it is intended to support arts educators—and educators in other curricular areas—who are interested in better understanding how their work can play a constructive role in youth social-emotional development.

The Consortium framework on developmental experiences and relationships suggests that arts education does provide particularly rich opportunities for social-emotional development. Arts educators have an important role to play in social-emotional development, in part, because arts education is commonly believed to provide different ways of accessing and developing social-emotional competencies (e.g., empathy, perseverance, self-awareness) than is the case in other academic areas. That is, these commonly held cultural beliefs about the arts as emotional and spiritual may cue particular competencies even more in arts-related settings than in other settings (e.g., a theatre class may be more likely than a math or history class to bring forth a student's more extroverted side).

---

[17] Nagaoka et al. (2015), p. 5.
[18] Farrington et al. (2012); Farrington, Porter, & Klugman (forthcoming).
[19] Allensworth et al. (2018).
[20] Cantor et al. (2018); Richardson (2017).

Josefa Ortiz De Dominguez Elementary School

What is Arts Education?

For the purposes of this paper, we define "arts education" as teaching and learning in one or more art forms. Though we focus on what happens in formal and informal classroom instruction, this definition also includes informal teacher-student interactions, peer-to-peer settings, and even self-directed learning. We see "arts education" as an umbrella term that encompasses a wide variety of disciplines, art forms, and practices. In Illinois, these are currently defined as:

 Visual arts

 Music

 Dance

 Theatre

 Media arts

illinoisartslearning.org[B]

B At other points in history, art forms have been aligned in different ways. For example, the main operative distinction between art forms throughout much of the 20th century was between fine arts and performing arts; music and math were closely aligned in the medieval university curriculum.

Art Practices and Social-Emotional Components

To better understand *how* the developmental experiences of arts education may provide opportunities for social-emotional development, we must first unpack the umbrella term of **"arts education."** To do this productively, we must look beyond the common preliminary step of specifying the main arts discipline in which an experience occurs. Rather, to understand how arts education can impact social-emotional development, we argue it is first necessary to be quite specific in describing the art practices that make up an arts education experience. It is these art practices that have the potential to foster social-emotional development.[21]

Art practices are the individual activities that students engage in as part of an arts process, class, or experience, including action experiences (encountering, tinkering, choosing, practicing, and contributing) and reflection experiences (describing, evaluating, connecting, envisioning, and integrating). We use the term *art practices* to refer to the particular art-related experiences a young person has in a given moment in a given setting, as opposed to the educational experience and broader curricular goals of which that art practice is a part. Examples of art practices might include learning a new brushstroke technique as part of a visual arts program, rehearsing a musical passage as part of an orchestra class, or going through a warm-up exercise in advance of a play rehearsal. Any art program will offer opportunities for students to engage in multiple art practices over time, and perhaps several different art practices even within one lesson.

Art practices can vary widely from one art form to another and from one phase of artistic development to another.[22] The particular art practices that might be relevant as warm-up exercises in preparation for a rehearsal of Shakespeare's *Much Ado About Nothing* might be very different from those that are relevant in preparation for a rehearsal of August Wilson's *Fences*. The art practices students engage in during a painting class may be entirely different than either of these. Art practices also vary depending on a participant's age and level of experience in the art form—much different practices are relevant for first-graders than for seniors in high school.[23]

The list of art practices that may be part of a curriculum is vast. For illustrative purposes, we summarize this list in Figure 1 using the four major artistic processes defined in the National Core Arts Standards (creating, performing/presenting/producing, responding, and connecting) and the five arts disciplines that are part of the Illinois Arts Learning Standards (visual arts, music, dance, theatre, and media arts).[24]

FIGURE 1. ART PRACTICES

	CREATING	PERFORMING/PRESENTING/PRODUCING	RESPONDING	CONNECTING
THEATRE	●	●	●	●
DANCE	●	●	●	●
VISUAL ARTS	●	●	●	●
MUSIC	●	●	●	●
MEDIA ARTS	●	●	●	●

---

[21] Notwithstanding the importance of specificity, we use the term "arts education" in this report in recognition of the reality that the concept has become an organizing principle for an entire field of practice and research.

[22] Becker (2008).

[23] The College Board, *Child Development and Arts Education: A Review of Current Research and Best Practices* (2012) discusses recommendations for developmentally appropriate pedagogical approaches to arts education.

[24] Released in 2014, the National Core Arts Standards is process that guides educators in providing a unified quality arts education for students in Pre-K through high school (see https://www.nationalartsstandards.org/); the Illinois Arts Learning Standards is Illinois' implementation of arts learning standards that reflect best practices and identify what is important for students to know and be able to do in dance, media arts, music, theatre, and visual arts (see http://illinoisartslearning.org).

Building on the idea that, at its core, human learning is a deeply, fundamentally social and emotional process, we argue that each art practice[25] has a **social-emotional component.** The social-emotional component is the relational, meaning-making, and self-management aspect of the art process, class, or experience that can be shaped by both action experiences (encountering, tinkering, choosing, practicing, and contributing) and opportunities for reflection (describing, evaluating, connecting, envisioning, and integrating).[26] The social-emotional component is a distinctive characteristic of the art practice that provides opportunities for students to develop and exercise particular **social-emotional competencies** while engaging in that art practice.

Just as the list of art practices that may be part of a curriculum is vast, so is the list of social-emotional components of those art practices. For illustrative purposes, and as explained in more detail in Chapter 2, we summarize in Figure 2 three main domains of social-emotional competencies that are developed and exercised through the social-emotional components of art practices: self-management and discipline (intrapersonal); social and relationship skills (interpersonal); and self-expression and identity.

FIGURE 2. SOCIAL-EMOTIONAL COMPETENCIES

SELF-MANAGEMENT AND SELF-DISCIPLINE	INTERPERSONAL AND RELATIONSHIP SKILLS	SELF-EXPRESSION AND IDENTITY

In much the same way an art practice provides opportunities for young people to build one or more art competencies, the social-emotional component of that art practice provides opportunities for young people to build one or more social-emotional competencies. For example, the art practice of peer critique of students' self-portraits in a visual arts class might have complementary social-emotional components such as opportunities to develop listening skills, practice at communicating clearly with peers, and manage emotions. The art practice of learning a new brushstroke technique might have complementary components that build social-emotional competencies such as building self-control, focusing one's attention, and building self-confidence and a positive identity.

Each art practice has a social-emotional component; it is simultaneously an arts activity AND a social-emotional activity.

These examples illustrate that, in the same way art practices can vary widely from one art form to another, the complementary social-emotional components of these art practices can vary as well. Any individual art practice may afford opportunities to work on several social-emotional components, depending on the circumstances and the way that art practice is framed by the arts instructor or understood by the student. And, as with the art practices themselves, the connected social-emotional components also depend in part on the age of the learners.[27] We can visualize these connections for an art practice associated with a theatre performance as shown in Figure 3.

FIGURE 3. EACH ART PRACTICE HAS SOCIAL-EMOTIONAL COMPONENT(S)

SOCIAL-EMOTIONAL COMPONENT (Interpersonal and Relationship Skills)

ART PRACTICE (Theatre, Performing)

SOCIAL-EMOTIONAL COMPONENT (Self-Expression and Identity)

Art Education Process

At any given moment, a particular art practice and its complementary social-emotional components are the things students *do*. We observe students practicing a new sculpting technique and see that, in the process, they practice concentration and focus. Or we observe students rehearsing a scene in a play multiple times and, in the process, observe them learning and practicing how to identify and respond to others' emotions. Each of these moments is part of a larger **art education process** in which the learner is participating. By this, we mean the broader arc or cycle of artistic activity at the level of a program, curriculum, or course.

As illustrated in Figure 4, each large-scale art education process—creating a mural, staging a play, performing a dance piece—is made up of many small-scale art practices: painting a figure's eyes, rehearsing a scene, learning a dance step. Thus we would use "art education

---

[25] While we focus on arts education in this research and discuss ways in which the arts may be unique in this regard, we also recognize that the same could be said of other developmental experiences.
[26] Best (1978).

[27] *Foundations for Young Adult Success: A Developmental Framework* discusses the ways in which children of different ages are ready to learn and grow in different developmental areas (Nagaoka et al., 2015).

process" to describe the full arc of working with a group of students on the planning and executing of a school mural project or the choreography, practicing, and performing of a new dance program.

These small-scale art education practices and larger-scale art education processes are particular instances of developmental experiences. As such, they may also be iterative: each small practice and each larger process can build on the ones that came before. They are likely to be mutually reinforcing and cumulative. Over time, these many interlocking layers of art and social-emotional learning yield a multi-textured set of outcomes and points of inflection—moments where students have opportunities to learn new skills and make new choices that, with continued repetition and practice, may turn into ingrained skills and habits of mind.

Art and Social-Emotional Competencies

If art practices and their accompanying social-emotional components are the things students *do* in the context of an art education process, we can think of art competencies and social-emotional competencies as longer-term outcomes of that process—the skills and ingrained habits of mind that students *develop* (to a greater or lesser degree) through their participation in that art education process. An **art competency** refers to the artistic knowledge and skills a student develops as a result of their participation in an art education process and/or practice over time. For example, students who participate in a series of auditions, rehearsals, and performances as part of a chorus will engage in multiple art practices along the way. Each of these will contribute to them developing a new set of art competencies; following the prior example, these might include vocal range, stage presence, and the ability to perform in front of a crowd.

The main focus of our interest here, however, is the **social-emotional competencies** that students develop as the result of longer-term participation in an art education process. A social-emotional competency is a set of one or more social or emotional skills, beliefs, habits, or behaviors that has been reinforced as the result of repeated developmental experiences (social-emotional components) during an art education process. That is, the social-emotional components of art practices, repeated over time and in varied contexts, will have an effect on the social-emotional competencies that students have at the conclusion of an art education process.

FIGURE 4. ART EDUCATION PROCESSES ARE COMPRISED OF MULTIPLE ART PRACTICES

CHAPTER 1 | Arts Education and Social-Emotional Learning: A Theory of Action

FIGURE 5. THEORY OF ACTION FOR ART EDUCATION AND SOCIAL-EMOTIONAL COMPETENCIES

Art Practices: CREATING | PRESENTING | RESPONDING | CONNECTING

Social-Emotional Components: SELF-MANAGEMENT AND SELF-DISCIPLINE | INTERPERSONAL AND RELATIONSHIP SKILLS | SELF-EXPRESSION AND IDENTITY

ART EDUCATION PROCESS: VISUAL ARTS

ART COMPETENCY

SOCIAL-EMOTIONAL COMPETENCY

The social-emotional components of an art practice amount to opportunities for young people to bring forth and exercise a set of social-emotional competencies. The result of this exercise is a change (hopefully an improvement) in those competencies. For example, we earlier described a visual arts class in which peer critique (an art education practice) offered students opportunities to develop listening skills, practice at communicating clearly with peers, and manage emotions. We would expect that, after participating in several such peer critiques, students' social-emotional competencies would be further developed and students would be more able to employ these competencies. The students would, at least to some degree, be *different* as listeners, speakers, and as people who can understand and respond constructively to others' emotions.

The mechanism for arts education to develop social-emotional competencies is through the social-emotional components of the art practices that comprise an art education process.

The illustration of these concepts in Figure 5 also acknowledges (through the bidirectional arrow between art competencies and social-emotional competencies) that not only are social-emotional competencies affected by participation in the arts, but art competency may also depend on social-emotional competency. That is, social-emotional and artistic competencies are mutually reinforcing; artistic competencies both affect and are affected by one's competencies in the social-emotional realm. For example, students' artistic skills and identities as artists have an impact on the way they interact with the world from a social-emotional perspective. At the same time, students pursuing technically demanding art forms may require significant self-discipline, self-regulation, and perseverance to master the competencies required by that art form. Students pursuing art forms that emphasize personal voice and expression need to find ways to access, work with, and express their emotions and experiences in the context of their artistic practice. Arts education provides a particular avenue for social-emotional development, and social-emotional competencies, in turn, contribute to one's developing artistic skills and knowledge.

The empirical literature and the participants in our interviews tended to focus almost exclusively on the positive impact that arts education has on social-emotional development. Indeed, many of the stakeholders we interviewed described specific expectations about how arts education would serve as a social-emotional "technology" to help students work on specific areas of development. For example, some parents saw theatre classes as a way to increase their shy children's self-confidence in public speaking. Music instructors emphasized the value in practicing an instrument as a mechanism for developing self-discipline or the benefits for interpersonal skills in being part of an orchestra. And parents, students, and visual arts teachers all described ways they believed painting and drawing would afford opportunities for self-expression, exploration of personal interests, and stress relief.

We can think of these kinds of changes in social-emotional competencies—changes that support young people's development and contribute to their ability to eventually meet the complex expectations and demands of adulthood—as being positive. However, the impact of an arts experience on social-emotional competencies can also be more negative if it acts as an impediment to future development or makes life more difficult (e.g., increased anxiety or feelings of inadequacy, shame, or isolation).

The relevant question is not *if* an art practice will affect a social-emotional competency, but *how* it will happen and what arts educators can do to improve the odds that the impact is positive.[28] This theory therefore highlights the importance of educators intentionally and consciously helping students take advantage of the opportunities to practice social-emotional components of an art practice and guide them toward improved social-emotional competencies based on their arts experiences.

Cultural Beliefs about Arts Education

The dynamic relationship between arts education and social-emotional development described in this theory of action doesn't happen in a vacuum; the cultural beliefs students, instructors, and others bring to particular learning settings influence every aspect of the process we describe here, from the social-emotional components that are the most likely complements to particular art practices, to the art practices that are likely to comprise an art education process, to the meaning that arts instructors or learners ascribe to their arts experiences. Such cultural beliefs both shape and are shaped by the larger community and social contexts in which arts education happens.[29]

---

[28] Bartel & Cameron (2002, April 3).

[29] Goffman (1974).

This research surfaced some important ways in which cultural beliefs about the role of the arts and of arts education may shape the actual connections between arts education and social-emotional learning. In a different time and place, with a different set of cultural beliefs about the role of the arts, some of these perceived connections between the arts and social-emotional competencies might be quite different. But in the context in which we conducted this research, we noted a widespread belief among parents, students, educators, and others that the arts—generally, or a particular art form or artistic practice—can play a special role in social-emotional development.

Beliefs about this special role of the arts were rooted, both in the research literature and among many of those we spoke with, in the Romantic ideal of art as being about "the beautiful and the sublime," and uniquely capable of facilitating emotional expression and spiritual transcendence. Many arts educators, parents, and even students spoke in some way of the idea that "art is about emotions." These beliefs about the access that arts education gives to the emotional or spiritual realm are in contrast to the beliefs we heard about what other academic subjects were about, and this shared viewpoint could strengthen the pathway between developmental experiences in the arts and social-emotional development.

One of the most consistent elements of effective arts instruction that emerged in our research is the practice of teachers creating a "safe space" in which students can participate in the arts.[30] Many arts educators operate on the belief that arts participation requires an environment in which students feel comfortable taking productive risks, being challenged, feeling discomfort, and growing emotionally. While there may be no single answer or "key" to how this is done, safe spaces are rooted in consciously and intentionally created environments of trust. Creating safe, developmental spaces may also involve educators finding opportunities to facilitate student agency and to be responsive to student desire: Where can arts learners make meaningful choices? Where can developing artists get excited about the learning process and make it their own? Where do students feel comfortable expressing themselves with trusted adults and peers? All of these features of arts education settings tend to play prominently in how arts teachers view their role.

FIGURE 6. CULTURAL BELIEFS INFLUENCE THE ARTS EDUCATION PROCESS

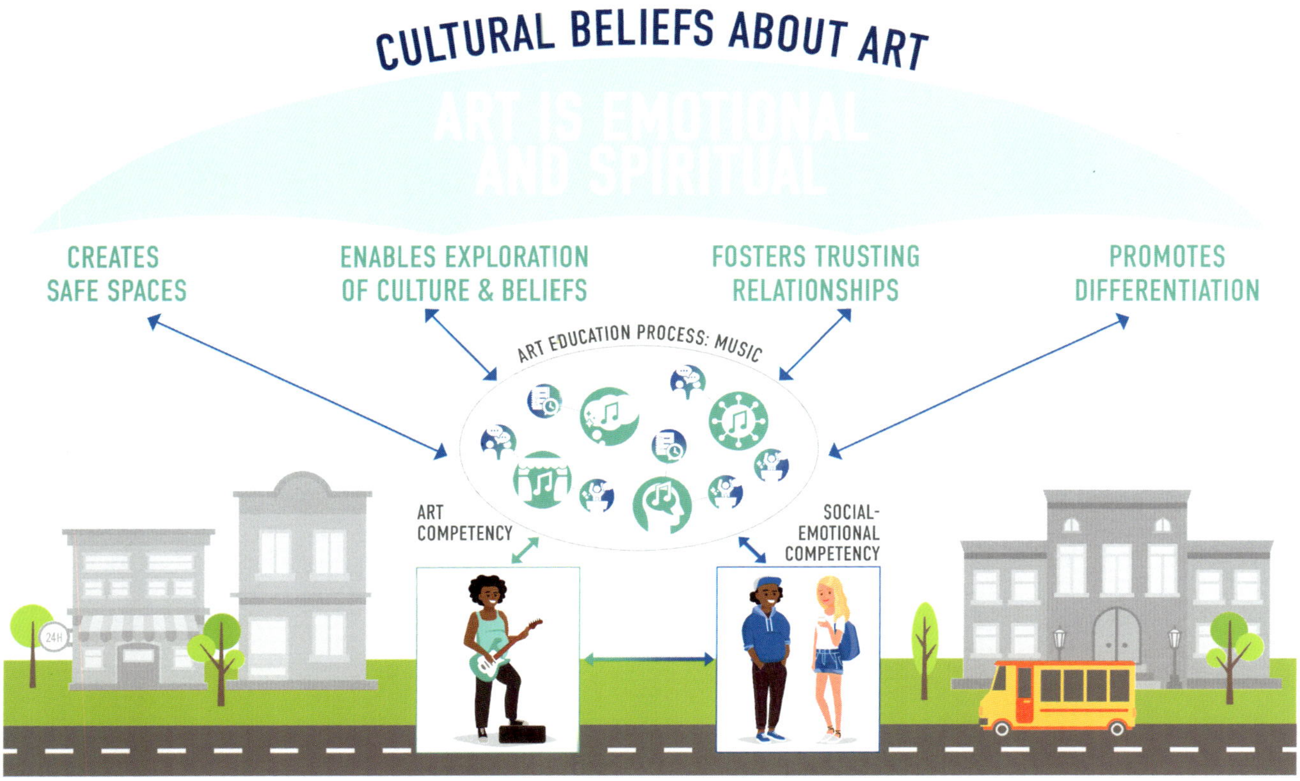

CULTURAL BELIEFS ABOUT ART

ART IS EMOTIONAL AND SPIRITUAL

CREATES SAFE SPACES

ENABLES EXPLORATION OF CULTURE & BELIEFS

FOSTERS TRUSTING RELATIONSHIPS

PROMOTES DIFFERENTIATION

ART EDUCATION PROCESS: MUSIC

ART COMPETENCY

SOCIAL-EMOTIONAL COMPETENCY

---

30 Macy (2004); Freeman, Sullivan, & Fulton (2003); McBride & Maurer (2016).

There are also significant, though not universal, differences between the way the arts are taught compared to other subjects. Many teaching artists identified a strong connection between art and the idea of **exploring the culture and beliefs** of oneself and of others. For example, some arts educators make pedagogical choices to emphasize the connection between art and culture, making arts education a vehicle for cultural expression. Arts education thus can provide a venue for young people to explore and express their cultural identity while also enhancing their engagement and building their knowledge and appreciation of other cultures.[31] Relatedly, some arts educators also view the arts as an opportunity to engage social justice themes and as a means of making critical commentary on society. Movement and embodiment are also accepted and often welcomed in arts settings, in part because personhood, identity, and emotions are central to many types of arts teaching and learning.[32]

Differentiation among student needs to teach a common set of skills is a key element of good teaching in any subject. Perhaps because of the absence of standardized testing and standardized curriculum, as well as a strong belief among arts instructors that the arts are adaptable to different needs, interests, personalities, and abilities, differentiation emerged as especially relevant in the arts. Arts instructors in this project emphasized the importance of meeting students where they are, holding this kind of flexibility as a core value of quality arts teaching and learning.

Collectively, these themes in how the arts are taught today can facilitate a special kind of relationship between students and art educators and between students and their peers. Both the research literature[33] and many of those we spoke to reported that students have more **trusting relationships** with their art educators than with other types of teachers, and feel comfortable in their arts classes disclosing and working through challenging situations they may be facing. For certain students, the depth of enjoyment that they get from art and the relationships they have with their art educators may motivate them to stay involved in arts learning (and may motivate them to stay engaged in school more generally). In some cases, a passion for one or more art forms also has important effects on the relationships that a student has with peers and adults, and this shift in relationships may in turn affect not only social-emotional competencies, but other student outcomes as well. For example, some parents and classroom teachers spoke of seeing particular children in a new light after observing their music, dance, or theatre performance. These data suggest that the experience of seeing a child as talented in one setting may lead an adult away from a deficit perspective to instead focus on that child's potential.

"Kids just have to have outside interests... I think having that identity is what contributes to confidence and growth and the social side of life and interpersonal skills...I feel like you could have this same conversation about... math or English, depending on how those classes are structured."

So are the arts different? Do the arts have a special role to play in social-emotional development among young people? Regardless of whether the theory presented here describes the actual effect of "art itself" on social-emotional learning or the effect of cultural and contextual beliefs about what art is and what it can do, educators in all contexts can learn much from the ways that many arts educators leverage the rich set of affordances for social-emotional learning described in this report. Indeed, many instructional frameworks already embed ideas like the ones discussed here in their definitions of good teaching in any subject.[34]

---

31 Ladson-Billings (1994).
32 This is, of course, not always the case. Adult expectations of behavior are often situated within White, mainstream social norms that may differ from some students' perceptions and experiences, and arts can be taught in a manner that alienates students of color by upholding social and cultural norms about what is and is not art or by elevating particular art forms or practices over others.
33 Deasy (2002); Fiske (1999); Hoxie & Debellis (2014).
34 For example, the CPS Framework for Teaching (https://www.ctunet.com/rights-at-work/text/2013-CPS-Framework-for-Teaching-w-Critical-Attributes_20130930.pdf) includes many of these concepts in its definition of Proficient and Distinguished teaching.

A theatre teaching artist noted, in reflecting on the way in which her work might affect students socially and emotionally, that "One of the hardest things in class is showing up, just showing up." So she designed an activity around "showing up": having each student stand up, one by one, while the other students clapped, and recite a line using a "performance voice." At the end of the activity, a classroom teacher approached the theatre teaching artist, so moved that she herself could barely speak, and said, "That child doesn't talk." The teaching artist noted that this was normal—sometimes students did not wish to talk in front of their peers. The classroom teacher replied "No, you don't understand, it's on his IEP. We try to get him to speak, he doesn't speak. He has elective mutism." But in the context of this theatre activity, he chose to use his voice.

Forward Momentum Dance

CHAPTER 2

Exploring Arts Education and Social-Emotional Learning in Practice

What does the connection between arts education and social-emotional learning look like in practice? To help illustrate this theory and some possible connections between arts education and social-emotional learning, we discuss in this section the empirical evidence from extant research literature and our Chicago fieldwork.

In both the literature and our fieldwork, three domains of social-emotional competencies seemed most prevalent, so we use these to organize this discussion:
- Self-management and discipline (intrapersonal)
- Social and relationship skills (interpersonal)
- Self-expression and identity

Together, these three domains comprise the social-emotional competencies (see Figure 2 on page 15)—the cognitive, social, and emotional skills, beliefs, and behaviors—that enable young people to interact productively with others, build and express a healthy sense of self and community, and work effectively toward their goals. The first two domains align with the intrapersonal (self-management)/interpersonal (social-relational) distinction made by the National Research Council in its study, *Education for Life and Work*.[35] These are also consistent with the categorization by Collaborative on Academic, Social, and Emotional Learning (CASEL), which links self-awareness and self-management, and then social awareness and relationship skills, as four of their five core social-emotional competencies.[36] Our third domain of "self-expression and identity" aligns with the "integrated identity" component of the UChicago Consortium's *Foundations for Young Adult Success* framework.[37] These human competencies are interrelated and mutually reinforcing; developing competence in one area supports development in another. Studies of the effects of arts education in our literature review commonly looked at outcomes across these three domains, and these were most often mentioned by participants in focus groups and interviews with students, arts educators, parents, and arts program administrators in Chicago.

While this section draws on the empirical evidence from the research literature and our Chicago fieldwork, it is not a "test" of our theory. We do not attempt in this section to specify every potential link between arts education and social-emotional learning. Nor do we review the individual studies that comprise the research on arts education on social-emotional learning. Much of this research is descriptive (describing arts programs and describing the kinds of benefits that participants believed they gained from participating) with little rigorous experimental evidence. Rather, we aim in this section to explore what we know and hypothesize about some of these links and, in the process, to provide examples that illustrate ways the theory can help practitioners be more thoughtful and creative in taking advantage of opportunities for social-emotional growth that arts education affords.

Self-Management and Self-Discipline

Self-management and self-discipline describe the skills students require to take responsibility for their own behavior and well-being and to pursue the goals that they set. While self-discipline connotes making oneself do something one must do, self-management includes recognizing, "owning," and being able to direct one's own emotions, behaviors, and attention toward one's desired purposes. Self-regulation, metacognition (thinking about thinking), motivation, responsibility,

---

35 National Research Council (2012).
36 CASEL's fifth core competency is "responsible decision-making."
37 Nagaoka et al. (2015).

perseverance, and "grit" are among the social-emotional competencies that fit most clearly within this domain.

Researchers, arts education practitioners, parents, and even students describe a variety of ways in which art education processes may promote improved self-management and self-discipline. For example, learning in arts education often requires extensive practice to meet the exacting requirements of a particular art form. To play an instrument, you must learn to use your hands, mouth, and/or breath to form the notes. To perform *Swan Lake*, you must first learn the names and shapes of basic ballet positions and be able to conform your body to them. Developing basic competence requires focused effort and repetition, and developing mastery requires years of dedicated practice. For an area of education often perceived as recreational, arts education can be highly demanding. But such exactitude has payoffs. Sam,[38] an elementary school student whose mother felt that taking piano lessons was important for him to develop self-management skills, pointed out the ways in which arts education pressed on him the need to do things the right way. He said, *"It changes the way I think, because I used to think, 'Oh if I could get this done really quickly and find the shortest solution.' I think it has changed my brain, like 'Take your time on it, and do it correct, and figure it out instead of just going through it quickly.'"* He also contrasted the arts education context—specifically his art class—to other subject areas—specifically math—saying, *"Painting you can't really have shortcuts. You have to take your time with it...But for math, there's always shortcuts that people find, so I don't think you have to put in as much focus as you do with painting."*

Evergreen Academy Middle School

[38] All names from our fieldwork are pseudonyms.

VIGNETTE #1
Piano and Personal Growth

Angela, a music educator in Chicago, was working with one of her middle school students, Monique, to prepare for a piano recital. Monique had previously dealt with a variety of anxiety-related issues, several of which rose to the surface during the recital preparations. Angela recognized this as an opportunity for Monique to practice dealing with her anxiety in a new context.

Angela normalized Monique's anxiety, noting that all musicians face this challenge. Then, the two imagined *"What if the worst case scenario happens, and you completely blank out, you walk off stage, you can't do it. The next morning you wake up, the earth is still turning, things are still the same, nobody really talks about it, everybody forgot about it."* Angela also gave Monique breathing and mindfulness practices to use leading up to the recital.

These conversations also brought to mind a strategy Monique had used to overcome anxiety during basketball games, which she called *"getting inside the game."* Angela helped Monique transfer this approach to music by discussing *"Paying attention to your goals musically, technically, what kind of posture are you going to sit with, paying attention to the physicality of the performance, paying attention to the rise and fall of the melodic line."*

On the day of the recital, the student who performed before Monique experienced severe anxiety during the performance. Instead of being overcome by anxiety herself, Monique was able to be compassionate and empathetic toward this other student in a way that helped her to activate her anxiety-coping strategies. Monique ended up having a successful recital performance.

- **Art Education Process:** Middle school student taking piano lessons

- **Art Practice:** Preparing for and then performing in a piano recital

- **Social-Emotional Components:** Dealing with performance anxiety using breathing and mindfulness practices; focusing on the details of the art practice as a way of removing anxiety-provoking distractions; practicing compassion and empathy for others

- **Social-Emotional Competencies:** Improved skills for self-management and self-regulation; ability to transfer social-emotional competencies from one domain to another; compassion and empathy for others

- **Takeaway for Teachers:** Art practices may activate students' underlying social and emotional challenges, but can provide a novel context in which to productively work through these challenges using new strategies. By being attuned to the ways in which art practices draw upon students' underlying personal needs, issues, and characteristics, educators can find ways to use the challenge of the experience to intentionally and consciously promote creative personal and interpersonal growth.

CHAPTER 2 | Exploring Arts Education and Social-Emotional Learning in Practice

Music

Art Practices:

PERFORMING	RESPONDING	CONNECTING

Social-Emotional Components:

SELF-MANAGEMENT AND SELF-DISCIPLINE	INTERPERSONAL AND RELATIONSHIP SKILLS	SELF-EXPRESSION AND IDENTITY

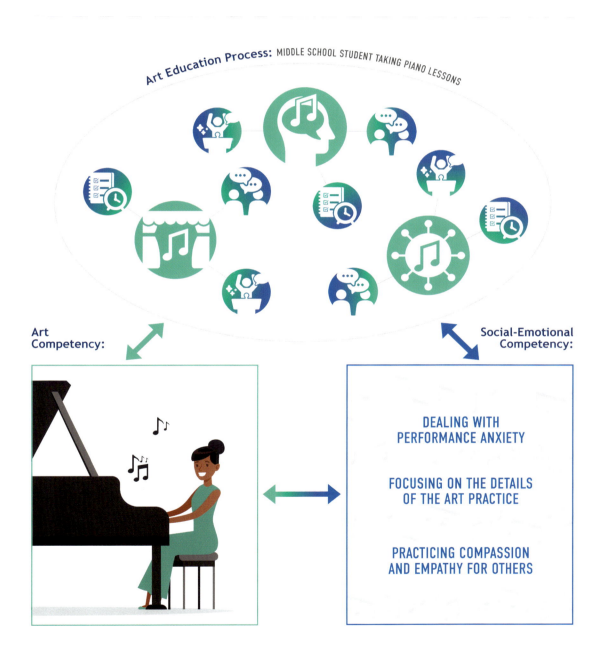

Art Education Process: MIDDLE SCHOOL STUDENT TAKING PIANO LESSONS

Art Competency:

Social-Emotional Competency:

DEALING WITH PERFORMANCE ANXIETY

FOCUSING ON THE DETAILS OF THE ART PRACTICE

PRACTICING COMPASSION AND EMPATHY FOR OTHERS

Arts education can also serve as a forum for rehearsing emotions that students will both experience and need to manage in their real lives. Larson and Brown (2007) theorized that arts programs "are important settings for understanding emotional development, first, because they are typically contexts of instrumental goal-directed activity and thus may help prepare adolescents for the emotional dynamics of adult work settings."[39] A theatre student in Chicago discussed the experience of rehearsing and then performing in front of a live audience, and the way these experiences helped to develop their emotional repertoire. *"It's definitely different during rehearsals and then the actual show. Like, your attitude is very different, I think. In rehearsals, you want to do your best and try your hardest, but in the actual performance when there's a live audience and everybody's there.... You kind of have to force yourself to be in the situation, like someone else's shoes, but putting yourself into an imaginary person's shoes. There's a quote on the wall, I forget who it's by, but it's like, acting is reacting truthfully to imaginary situations, or something like that, I don't know. But it's really interesting because it's true, you're in a fake situation, but you have to act how your character would really act."*

Many programs in the literature advocate for an arts-integration model, in which the arts are integrated into core subject areas, such as history or language arts. Integration practices include activities such as acting out a story which might mirror a real-world dilemma[40] or drawing pictures for a story a student writes.[41] Through these activities, students have the opportunity to "rehearse" emotions—sometimes from other people's perspectives, sometimes from their own—which may improve self-regulation. Brown and Sax (2013) reported, in their mixed-methods study of an arts-integrated preschool program, that children participating in the program "showed greater growth in teacher-rated levels of positive and negative emotion regulation."[42] Other studies have shown that the self-regulatory benefits of arts education can transfer to other domains.[43]

Self-management and self-discipline are not simply skills to "make oneself" do something that is beneficial but unpleasant. Broader research on achievement motivation shows clearly that human beings work hard at things they care about and for which they feel some opportunity for choice and autonomy.[44] Therefore, arts settings can provide opportunities for young people to experience the benefits of working hard by giving them ownership over that work. This ownership can exist for a variety of reasons, including an emphasis on the process (rather than the product);[45] allowing students to imbue art works with emotion or personal meaning;[46] or having students serve as creators of art, rather than mere appreciators.[47] Larson and Brown's (2007) study of the student production of *Les Misérables* found that students "almost always framed the learning process as one in which they were the agents of change."[48] Harman and Smagorinsky (2014) observed that the Latina students participating in a Boalian theatrical intervention,[49] which included improvisation, writing, storytelling, and drawing, "seemed highly motivated because they had selected the topics, chosen how to reach their audience, and received instruction on how to develop informational texts."[50]

Feeling motivated is key to self-management. Sam, the student who compared the rigors of his painting class to that of his math class, confirms the importance of this ownership, noting, *"I like painting, I like bringing the artwork to my house, like showing it off…you can show your emotions through it. So you go there, you paint what you want to paint."* Perhaps this sense of ownership fueled Sam's improved self-management and discipline in doing his work without seeking shortcuts.

Of course, arts education is not always connected to positive social-emotional outcomes. Art practices present many opportunities to develop improved competencies at self-management and self-discipline, but this outcome is not a foregone conclusion. For example, while some students may develop perseverance and grit when they are made to practice an instrument, the same experience in other students may create feelings of resentment and hostility and create perceptions among parents or teachers of laziness or defiance. Students may

---

39 Larson & Brown (2007).
40 Brouillette et al. (2014); Collins & Cooper (1997); Hetland & Winner (2004); McCammon, Saldaña, Hines, & Omasta (2012); Ross Goodman (1990), as cited in Deasy (2002); Walsh-Bowers & Basso (1999); Williamson & Silvern (1992), as cited in Deasy (2002).
41 Scripp (2007); Wilhelm (1995), as cited in Deasy (2002).
42 Brown & Sax (2013)
43 Alemán et al. (2016); Asbury & Rich (2008); McCammon et al. (2012).
44 Farrington et al. (2012).
45 Beales & Zemel (1990); Bergmann (1995); Blatner (1995); Catterall & Peppler (2007); Collins & Cooper (1997); Deasy (2002); Freeman et al. (2003); Gallagher, Ntelioglou, & Wessels (2013); Gullatt (2008); Hanna (2008); Harman & Smagorinsky (2014); Kahn (1999); Katz (2008); Kisiel, Blaustein, Spinazzola, Schmidt, Zucker, & van der Kolk (2006); Macy (2004); Mages (2010); Pellegrini & Galda (1982); Rose, Parks, Androes, & McMahon (2000); Runfola, Etopio, Hamlen, & Rozendal (2012); Ruppert (2006); Thomas, Signh, Klopfenstein (2015); Ulfarsdottir & Erwin (1990); Walker, McFadden, Tabone, & Finkelstein (2011); Walker, Tabone, & Weltsek (2011); Walsh-Bowers & Basso (1999); Zimmerman (2009); Zimmerman & Zimmerman (2000).
46 Bergmann (1995); Brown & Sax (2013); Catterall & Peppler (2007).
47 Asbury & Rich (2008); Baker & Homan (2007); Brinda (2008); Farnum & Schaffer (1998); Hoxie & Debellis (2014); Miksza (2013); Thomas et al. (2015); Ulfarsdottir & Erwin (1990).
48 Larson & Brown (2007), p. 1094.
49 Boalian theatrical interventions are named for Augusto Boal, the founder of Theatre of the Oppressed. It is not necessarily the objective of Theatre of the Oppressed to produce professional-grade drama, but rather to reimagine scenes representing oppression in participants' everyday lives. The work by Harman and Smagorinsky relies on an emphasis on the role of drama as both personal and educational, particularly with regard to students' political awareness and understanding of the agency they have opposing bigotry toward them and/or their communities.
50 Harman & Smagorinsky (2014).

learn to take shortcuts or use deception to get out of practicing. Over time, such feelings, judgments, and behaviors may create a negative feedback loop that leaves the young person doubting their own abilities or thinking of themselves in a negative light rather than learning to persevere through challenges.

Arts educators who are attentive to these possibilities can take care to ensure that opportunities for self-management are coupled with a concerted effort to make arts learning meaningful and engaging for students. Growing and succeeding in the arts demands practice, whether rehearsing scales, running lines, perfecting techniques, or any other repetitive task. But it is not always enough to tell students to practice. Educators can also consciously and intentionally identify practice as an opportunity to develop a social-emotional competency that can serve them in other endeavors going forward: that of dedicating one's self to improvement through focused practicing. Highlighting the personal stake a student can take in the activity can drive that student to a desire to "make perfect." And this quest for perfection can create a repeated cycle of rehearsal, often involving a variety of emotions, including frustration and satisfaction, which will come into play in the world outside of the arts.

Interpersonal and Relationship Skills

Interpersonal and relationship skills relate to students' abilities to understand others' feelings and perspectives, as well as the social and ethical norms which contribute to their ability to maintain healthy and rewarding relationships.[51] Relationship-building, teamwork, empathy, and perspective-taking are among the social-emotional competencies that fit within this domain.

Arts education is commonly believed by practitioners, students, and parents alike to aid in the development of young people's interpersonal and relationship skills.[52] Art education processes often include highly social activities that provide students with opportunities to express themselves, interact in novel ways, and work collectively, practicing and developing interpersonal skills such as collaboration, communication, and conflict resolution.[53] School-based arts classes or community arts programs often bring together youth from many different cultural backgrounds and experiences. As one Chicago high school student described, *"I mean theatre is a shared interest… [but not necessarily] a shared identity….There's a community with theatre, but it's more of a bonding through the long rehearsal hours rather than bonding over a shared identity."*

Developing their interpersonal skills can also aid students in getting the most benefit from their relationships with artists, peers, and others in their art education settings, increasing their ability to leverage social and cultural capital.[54] However, the extent to which these outcomes are realized is likely to vary both from one student to another and by how students' identities are acknowledged by teacher pedagogy and art form.[55] Learners need to feel that they can bring themselves fully into a setting and that they are seen and known in order to fully engage in learning.[56]

Of the various art education processes in which students may engage, those that involve performing are most commonly expected to foster interpersonal skills in students because of the importance of social involvement and peer-to-peer collaboration.[57] In a study of a theatre program, for example, one student reported, *"Socially I think it changed me. Like, because I am interacting with people doing something I like, I think it's—for some strange reason I think it has made me more open and able to talk with people my age and socialize a little more. Like before, I was very meek and I guess kinda shy like, I never really made friends? But then I finally, I just started to make some."*[58]

---

51 https://casel.org/core-competencies/
52 Allen & Boykin (1992), as cited in Brown & Sax (2013); Upitis & Smithrim (2003), as cited in Walker, McFadden, Tabone, & Finkelstein (2011); Ruppert (2006); Allison & Rehm (2007), as cited in Brown & Sax (2013); Barrett & Bond (2014); Richards (2011); Young (1990), as cited in Brown & Sax (2013); Hoxie & Debellis (2014); Thomas et al. (2015).
53 Barrett & Bond (2014); McCammon et al. (2012).
54 Foster & Marcus Jenkins (2017); Hoxie & Debellis (2014); Pulido (2009); Taliaferro Baszile (2009).
55 Eccles & Gootman (2002) ; Lerner et al. (2009), as cited in Rusk et al. (2013); Gaztambide-Fernandez (2013).
56 Allensworth et al. (2018); Osher et al. (2018).
57 Barrett & Bond (2014); Davis (2009); McCammon et al. (2012).
58 Wright, John, Alaggia, & Sheel (2006).

VIGNETTE #2
Les Misérables and Relationship-Building

In *Emotional Development in Adolescence: What Can Be Learned from a High School Theater Program* (2007),[C] Larson and Brown studied a group of high school students participating in their school's spring theatre production of *Les Misérables*. Over the course of three spring months leading up to the musical's performance, Larson and Brown conducted a series of interviews with parents, teachers, and a sample of 10 actors out of the group of 110 who were part of the production.

The students in the production described entering "a whole 'nother world" each day they came to the theatre for rehearsal. The culture of this world was consciously cultivated by the adult leaders of the program and included three central features that were designed to help students share in and learn from the emotion of the performance.

First, the adult leaders established and set high expectations for a commitment to the work of putting on the production. In doing so, they created a culture "in which this work and effort was not just expected, it was celebrated."

Second, the leaders recognized, accepted, and even modeled the strong emotions that they expected to be part of the process of preparing for the production. The modeling of emotions by the adult leaders was intentionally focused on enhancing constructive collaboration.

Third, the leaders established a culture that provided emotional support, intentionally and consciously encouraging cast and crew to be respectful and supportive of one another.

- **Art Education Process:** High school students rehearsed for a production of *Les Misérables*

- **Art Practice:** Rehearsing and performing scenes in preparation for a formal presentation of the production

- **Social-Emotional Components:** Working together to accomplish a goal with minimal adult supervision; experiencing regular successes and failures; having repeated opportunities to engage in challenging activities; observing peers going through all of the above

- **Social-Emotional Competencies:** Deeper understanding and awareness of one's own emotions; ability to recognize the emotional states of others; greater skill at recognizing the effects of emotion on behavior

- **Takeaway for Teachers:** The rehearsal process is an ideal setting for students to repeatedly engage with emotional experiences. These repeated opportunities allow students to practice working with emotions, at a remove from their personal experiences, and thus learn how to understand their own and their peers' emotional states and achieve better emotional regulation for self and group success.

C Larson & Brown (2007).

Theatre

Art Practices:

CREATING	PERFORMING	RESPONDING

Social-Emotional Components:

SELF-MANAGEMENT AND SELF-DISCIPLINE	INTERPERSONAL AND RELATIONSHIP SKILLS	SELF-EXPRESSION AND IDENTITY

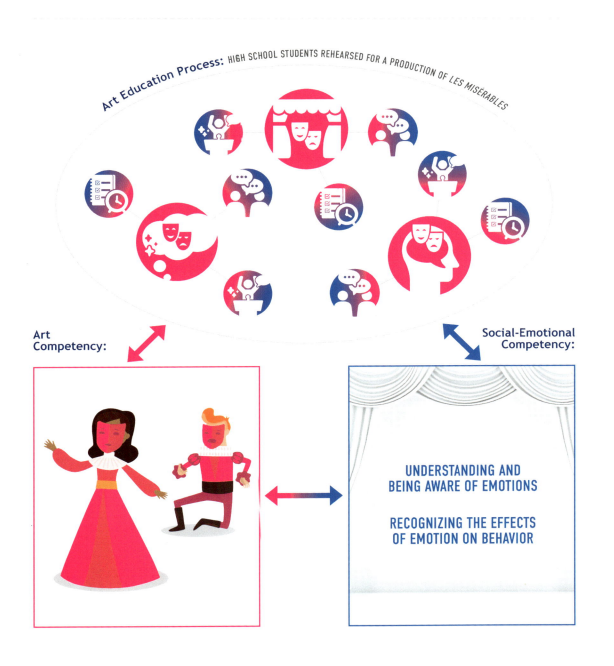

Art Education Process: HIGH SCHOOL STUDENTS REHEARSED FOR A PRODUCTION OF LES MISÉRABLES

Art Competency:

Social-Emotional Competency:

UNDERSTANDING AND BEING AWARE OF EMOTIONS

RECOGNIZING THE EFFECTS OF EMOTION ON BEHAVIOR

Some arts practitioners report that changes like this occur precisely because the opportunities to practice interpersonal skills are so intrinsically tied to the art forms.[59] For example, dance and theatre require students to move in synchrony with one another while following cues and choreography, drawing on verbal and nonverbal communication and spatial awareness of the self as well as others.[60] In his expansive compendium of studies on arts and learning, Deasy (2002) speculates that the act of engaging in fantasy play allows students to develop perspective-taking and conflict-resolution skills because of the common occurrence of conflict while students develop plots and characters. Baker and Homan (2007), in their study of a music program in a juvenile detention center that included rap, music sequencing, and production, attest to the opportunities offered to participants to engage in "individual and collective communication."[61] One participant, Laurence, reported, *"I shared my lyrics with someone to let them know how I express myself inside. I showed my talent with somebody else and enjoyed it. It made me feel good I shared my lyrics and you shared your skill with me and we both understood each other's way of living."* Laurence's experience perfectly illustrates the ways in which these interactions allow for an iterative and interlocking process that allows participants to practice, build, and expand their artistic, personal, and interpersonal repertoire.

Teamwork and accountability are also important elements of some arts education experiences that can provide opportunities for students to practice interpersonal and relationship skills. Alemán et al. (2016) examined El Sistema, a music curriculum that emphasizes social interactions through group instruction and group performances, finding that it improved self-control and reduced behavioral difficulties as students worked together to perform music. The authors also pointed out that "the skills that allow children to control their emotions and behavior during school age are closely related to skills used to secure and maintain good jobs and healthy relationships,"[62] signalling a transfer from the realm of arts education to other contexts, beyond the given art activity. This feeling of accountability to others may extend not just to the other members of a team, but to an audience as well. In their study of the student production of *Les Misérables*, Larson and Brown (2007) found that students "voiced a sense of responsibility to create a good performance for the audience."[63]

Extracurricular art activities that offer opportunities for students to conceptualize and lead projects and mentor or teach other students may also help develop interpersonal and relationship skills.[64] For example, the Youth Art Board at the Hyde Park Art Center is fundamentally designed to foster young people's ability to lead, design, and implement arts programs. Youth Art Board members are responsible for developing projects, managing budgets, and working with staff and teaching artists to carry out plans. Kiesel et al. (2006) found in their study of the effects of participating in a theatre program for "at-risk" students that students displayed increases of prosocial behaviors following the program. Lerner and Mikami (2012) found that participating in theatre games "improved social behavior and perspective taking" in youth with autism spectrum disorder.[65] In a study of student participation in a middle school music program, the researcher noted that "belongingness" seemed to be an important factor in students' experience, commenting that music "lends itself to social functions quite naturally."[66]

As is the case with self-management and self-discipline, arts educators can take advantage of many art practices by consciously and intentionally attending to the social-emotional components of those practices to develop interpersonal and relationship skills. For example, an art practice like rehearsing a scene in a theatre class will have social-emotional components, and these components are likely to provide students with opportunities to practice interpersonal and relationship skills like relationship-building, empathy, and teamwork. But the fact that these opportunities exist is no guarantee that the students will take away from them the kinds of lessons that ultimately contribute to their ability to develop healthy and rewarding relationships or to understand social and ethical norms. Educators can consciously and intentionally identify the rehearsal as an opportunity to develop these skills and discuss with them how such skills can serve them in other endeavors going forward.

---

59 McCammon et al. (2012); Aldridge (1995), as cited in Ulfarsdottir & Erwin (1999); Bunt (1997), as cited in Ulfarsdottir & Erwin (1999).
60 Hanna (2008); Gilbert (2002), as cited in Dow (2010); Sansom (2011).
61 Baker & Homan (2007).
62 Alemán et al. (2016), p. 446.
63 Larson & Brown (2007).
64 Green & Kindseth (2011); Hoxie & Debellis (2014), Interview.
65 Lerner & Mikami (2012), p. 1509.
66 Davis (2009).

Self-Expression and Identity

Social-emotional competencies related to self-expression and identity help students develop an integrated identity: the "internal compass that a young adult uses to make decisions consistent with her values, beliefs, and goals."[67] This internal compass enables students to maintain a sense of who they are across different contexts and to resolve conflicts between different aspects of the self (e.g., race/ethnicity, gender, age). An integrated identity also provides a foundation for other social-emotional competencies, regardless of how it is developed. As one Chicago elementary school parent described, *"I want [my daughter] to have an identity in high school. I don't care what it is, whether you're a basketball player or an artist or yearbook [editor], but something... And I think having that identity is what contributes to confidence and growth and the social side of life and interpersonal skills and all of that. ...it's kind of acclimating kids with other interests and getting them involved, and what that does for them socially and interpersonally and from a confidence perspective."*

There is widespread agreement among practitioners, students, and qualitative researchers that arts education in any art form can support this kind of self-expression and identity development. As one veteran dance teacher expressed, "My one recurring thought was that the most basic mission of dance in education (and this is true of all of the arts) is to leave all students touched by a sense of themselves as whole, moving, thinking, feeling, and culturally valued individuals."[68] One avenue through which this may happen is the opportunity many art practices present to draw upon personal experience. In arts education, more than traditional academic classes, the "content" is in large part drawn from students' own observations and lived experiences, as opposed to an entirely external body of knowledge to be acquired. As sculptor Stephen De Staebler described, "At the core of all artistic efforts is the concern to express and experience what it means to be human. To be human means more than to be able to think: It encompasses the integration of all the senses and faculties we associate with the human person."[69]

Theatre and dance classes are seen to be particularly powerful sites for identity development and self-expression because students are using their own bodies as the medium for conveying feelings and ideas. In a study of the effects of creative dance, Murray (1973) noted that dance provided "a primary medium for expression involving the total self (not just a part, like the voice) or totally separated from the physical self (like painting or sculpture). Dance and the movement that produces it is 'me' and, as such, is the most intimate of expressive media. A child's self-concept, his own identity and self-esteem are improved in relation to such use of his body's movements."[70]

Montessori School of Englewood

---

[67] Nagaoka et al. (2015), p. 2.
[68] Knowles (1993).
[69] De Staebler (1998), p. 24, as cited in Campbell (2006).
[70] Murray (1973), p. 5, as cited in Bergmann (1995).

VIGNETTE #3
Graffiti and Identity

Tom is a visual arts teacher in an elementary school in Chicago. He recently completed a lesson with his sixth-graders on graffiti art. As Tom describes, *"I wanted to not only teach them the differences of street art and vandalism and the right and wrong of everything, but I wanted them to choose a voice within their art. So they could choose a word or statement through that project and say something that they were feeling."*

The context for the lesson was important. The population of the school was almost entirely Latino, and, in Tom's words, *"I think there was a lot of fear around that time last year, when there was just a lot of things with immigration in Chicago, tracking people, we had students not showing up to class because of it."*

In the course of teaching this lesson, some of Tom's students began to feel more comfortable expressing their previously unspoken ideas and fears about this difficult topic. Tom's approach of asking the students to focus on finding a voice led the students to engage with their own identities in the current political context and think in new ways about how they can and do fit in their communities.

- **Art Education Process:** Classroom lesson on graffiti for sixth-grade students

- **Art Practice:** Students learning about expressing a voice within their art by choosing words or statements that they would want to express with graffiti

- **Social-Emotional Components:** Some students used the opportunity to express opinions on current events and the impact of those events on their lives—for example, with regard to anti-immigrant sentiment. In the words of the teacher, *"They were able to kind of put it [graffiti] out there and see that it can be acceptable, and in an art form that kind of does have a bad name, they can practice it, and learn it, and get some history about it, but also use it to speak their mind."*

- **Social-Emotional Competencies:** This was an isolated lesson, but it allowed students to express ideas and feelings about which they had not previously been open. This helped their teacher to know what they were anxious about, and to respond to that anxiety. The satisfaction of discussing ideas that they hadn't had an opportunity to express before also helped students to better understand the complex messages that graffiti artists are trying to communicate through their art form.

- **Takeaway for Teachers:** In the words of this teacher, *"That's one of the best examples of giving those students the ability to think for themselves. So they've worked on the technical aspects of the art, but then they can take that and use it for however they feel."* Self-expression is a widely used term, and it has the potential to become a meaningless cliché. However, this is a clear case where a teacher was able to combine the artistic lesson with an opportunity for students to articulate their opinions and anxieties about life—in this case, about current events.

CHAPTER 2 | Exploring Arts Education and Social-Emotional Learning in Practice

Visual Arts

Art Practices:

CREATING	RESPONDING	CONNECTING

Social-Emotional Components:

SELF-MANAGEMENT AND SELF-DISCIPLINE	INTERPERSONAL AND RELATIONSHIP SKILLS	SELF-EXPRESSION AND IDENTITY

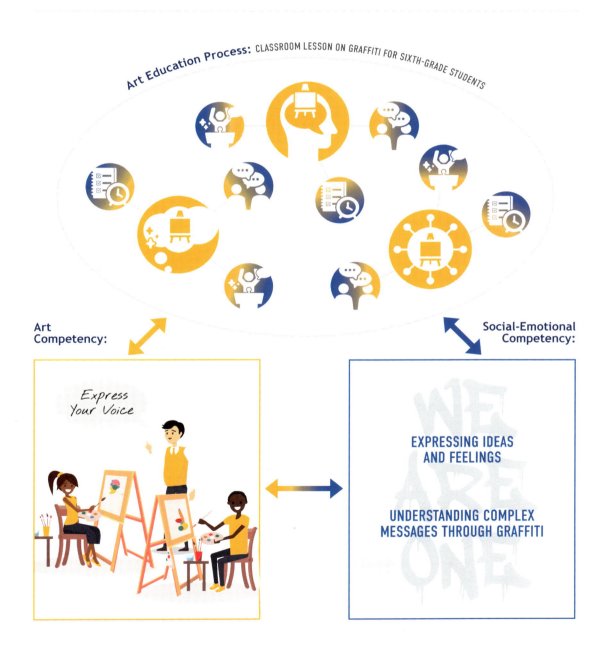

Art Education Process: CLASSROOM LESSON ON GRAFFITI FOR SIXTH-GRADE STUDENTS

Art Competency: Express Your Voice

Social-Emotional Competency:

EXPRESSING IDEAS AND FEELINGS

UNDERSTANDING COMPLEX MESSAGES THROUGH GRAFFITI

Particular art practices in any art form may call upon students to bring forth something from within themselves that is uniquely theirs. As one program administrator described, *"Arts gets to some place that I would call intrinsic. It sticks with you in a lot of ways and it's got an emotional connection in a way that is harder to get to in a math or science...When you ask students to participate in an art-making activity, you are asking them to participate in creating something and their voice gets to be a part of that...Even if I were to have a class of say, 15 students here and they were all to be doing a still-life drawing...None of them are going to be the same. Ever. And that is a beautiful thing! Whereas, you give 15 people a math exercise, you want them all to be the same...But with art...that is what we get [with] every art experience. Everybody is doing something completely different."*

This personal, emotional connection to the work can require students to take risks, risks that educators can use as opportunities for developing a more integrated sense of self. As one researcher noted after conducting a focus group with participants in a dance program, "It is striking that dance, a performing art, should turn out to accord these young women more occasions than their schools did to take the intellectual risks and exploratory chances necessary to achieve real growth. Such risk-taking also helps young people develop a durable sense of identity—one that is not fixed but that shifts in nuanced and thoughtful ways, responding spontaneously to the inevitably unpredictable nature of life…. For the young women I worked with, dance enabled them to become the people they aspired to be."[71]

In addition to the content of art classes drawing from students' own experience, art practices can be avenues for identity exploration and discovery. For example, in a study of 673 high school students in 14 vocal music ensembles, researchers surveyed students about their views on the meaning of their high school choral singing experience. "The results…lend support to the idea that musical experiences help individuals to discover their own identity or, as one participant in the pre-pilot study stated, 'to find out who I am.'"[72] Blatner (1995) argued that role playing within the context of theatre education "teaches people skills for participating in the creation of their own unfolding identities." In particular, "Role playing not only fosters the ability to relinquish one's egocentric viewpoint and…open imaginatively to the perspective of the other, but it also helps consolidate a deeper identity…."[73] Mitchell (2001) noted that hip-hop, with its four elements of MCing, DJing, graffiti writing, and breakdancing, constitutes processes through which identity is "actively imagined, created and constructed."[74]

Art processes may also promote self-expression and identity development when they are designed around the idea of exploring cultural identities that are more relevant to particular students than are dominant cultural norms. For example, research exploring Hip Hop Pedagogy suggests that artistic processes that capitalize on and value students' cultural backgrounds and racial, gender, sexuality, and class identities have been found to foster positive relationships and build social networks that empower young people and connect them with communities that support their personal inquiry and artistic expression.[75]

Presenting particular works of art focused on social justice issues to the public may also provide opportunities for young people to develop voice and identity, especially when these issues directly impact their lives. Harman and Smagorinsky (2014) describe how theatre for bilingual language learners and new immigrants served as a means to "reconstruct and depict a recurring social drama that had a profound impact on the students' senses of self and agency as immigrants in what they have found to be a hostile and forbidding environment." To perform this in public spaces as a form of civic engagement allowed students to promote change as it supported "young people's growing political awareness and understanding of the agency they have in contesting bigoted conduct toward them and their immigrant communities" and "supported students in reimagining and reinterpreting aspects of their personal, interpersonal, and institutional lives."[76]

In some cases, the connection between arts education and identity development may be more direct: students may come to identify as an artist or a creative person. As one student described, *"I made a tiny little pin cushion, and I was so happy. I brought it to school… I was like, you know, I sewed the button, I picked out the fabric, I cut it a certain way, I put them together, I did it inside-out, I stuffed it, I was really proud of myself. And it really does build confidence. …it makes you feel like, Wow I did this! I didn't know how to do this, but now I do. And I could tell people, oh yeah, I sew."*

---

[71] Katz (2008).
[72] Hylton (1981).
[73] Blatner (1995).
[74] Mitchell (2001), as cited in Baker & Homan (2007).
[75] Pulido (2009); Rodriguez (2009).
[76] Harmon & Smagorinsky (2014).

The social-emotional competencies that comprise the self-expression and identity domain are important contributors to a young person's development, and there are significant opportunities in arts education to promote growth of these competencies. This may be the domain in which it is most natural for arts educators to fully take advantage of these opportunities. As the examples provided in this section illustrate, arts educators often expect art practices to encourage students to express themselves and explore their own identity. Young people can also consciously and intentionally use many art practices as opportunities to take risks, engage with social and cultural issues, and reflect on their experiences, each of which can contribute to developing a more completely integrated identity.

Summary

Cultural beliefs about the arts often create an openness to consciously and intentionally exploring social-emotional development in ways that are not as accessible in other subject areas during the school day. Whether the link is between particular art practices and social-emotional competencies in the intrapersonal domain of self-management and self-discipline, the interpersonal domain of social and relationship skills, or the domain of self-expression and identity, art education processes can provide a wealth of opportunities for social-emotional learning.

However, arts education does not automatically lead to positive social-emotional development. Negative experiences in an art education process can, if not constructively engaged by arts educators, teach counterproductive social-emotional lessons. Students who have a bad experience in a live performance may, rather than learning grit or practicing perseverance, develop more severe anxiety around interpersonal or other communications. Without the supportive culture that arts educators seek to create, students whose artwork is misunderstood may, rather than developing a more integrated identity, develop less of a sense of self-worth.

Social-emotional development and meaning-making happen in arts education—indeed in all developmental experiences—regardless of whether the adults involved intentionally and consciously leverage the experiences to promote positive social-emotional outcomes. Rather than leaving the impact of arts experiences to chance, arts educators can foster positive social-emotional development by intentionally sequencing developmental experiences throughout art education processes, talking with students about their social and emotional experiences, and providing rich opportunities to reflect on those experiences in a supportive light.

Calmeca Folkloric Dances

CHAPTER 3

Conclusions and Implications

The theory presented in this project aims to describe how arts education can play a role in the development of social-emotional competencies that enable young people to interact productively with others, build and express a healthy sense of self and community, and work effectively toward their goals. The theory is flexible and generalized; we seek to provide a framework for arts educators—and educators in other curricular areas—to think about how to structure their work in ways that most constructively support the social-emotional development of children and youth.

Art practices and the social-emotional components of these practices are at the core of this theory. They are two ways of describing the same observable activity. For example, in a story related by a theatre teacher we spoke to, the activity of students standing up to perform lines in front of the class was an art practice—rehearsing how to deliver lines—with a corresponding social-emotional component: For one child with elective mutism, it was a new opportunity to try to speak, and for other children, perhaps a chance to build confidence and agency.

These core building blocks of art practices and their social-emotional components are nested within larger art education processes and are iterative in their effects. By "nested," we mean that each larger-scale education process (e.g., creating a mural, staging a play, performing a dance piece) is made up of many small-scale art practices (e.g., blending paint colors, rehearsing a scene, learning a dance step). By "iterative," we mean that each small-scale practice and each large-scale process builds on the ones that came before; they are mutually reinforcing and cumulative.

Over time and within a set of influential contexts (the immediate art setting, the school or organization, the neighborhood and community, the broader society), these many interlocking layers of art and social-emotional learning can contribute to the development of both art competencies and social-emotional competencies in young people. An art practice, repeated over time, is usually designed to improve students' art competencies. And the social-emotional components of the practice can, if repeated, lead to improved social-emotional competencies. For example, theatre students who have multiple opportunities to build confidence and agency through practicing of lines can, with constructive engagement by a supportive adult, gain in confidence and agency beyond the context of this particular art practice. In other words, art practices and related social-emotional components yield a set of outcomes and points of inflection—moments where students have opportunities to learn new skills and make new choices that, with continued repetition and practice, may turn into ingrained habits of mind and integrated parts of their identity.

What does all of this mean "on the ground?" One of our main objectives in describing the relationship between education in the arts and social and emotional learning outcomes is to provide practical suggestions for arts educators—indeed, for all educators—to bring back to their classrooms, studios, and performance spaces. In this section, we explore some of the most important implications of our research for educational practice.

Opportunity Is Critical to Development

A key takeaway for this project is applicable to both

arts educators and policymakers: healthy development depends on opportunity. Young people need a breadth of opportunities to thrive, from early childhood through young adulthood, and arts education should play a prominent role in cultivating that breadth.

Moreover, different types of activities are not interchangeable for individual students: some students love theatre, some love painting, others love a sport or math. Young people need access (geographic, financial, and culturally inclusive) to a wide range of high-quality activities—arts and non-arts, both in school and outside of school—so that they can find the ones that best suit them and ignite their passions.

This research was not designed to decipher what leads some kids to be interested in the arts more than sports, academics, or other extracurricular activities, much less what leads some kids to be particularly interested in one art form over another. What did become clear in the course of this project, however, is that young people and parents often view their arts education experiences as a critical and unique way for them to grow socially and emotionally.

For some students, a particular art discipline will "stick," and that art form will become a passion they devote their lives to. Simply by virtue of the amount of time, energy, and emotion they invest in this art, these students are likely to learn a wide range of social and emotional lessons along the way. But the theory presented here is not focused only on those students for whom an art form becomes a passion. Even for those for whom the arts don't "stick" in this way, whose attention is more focused on traditional academic subjects, sports, or some other extracurricular activity, exposure to arts education opportunities can still provide distinctive affordances for social-emotional learning. Like other learning outcomes, social-emotional learning is cumulative, so each social-emotional component is an opportunity for students to grow and build on what they've learned elsewhere.

Intentionality Ensures That Opportunities Are Fully Leveraged

One of the most important implications of this work for educational practice is that educators need to be intentional about the holistic development of their students. While the arts can provide a wealth of opportunities to encourage the development of social and emotional skills, our research highlights the important role an arts educator plays in drawing out the potential of these opportunities. Arts education is not a "black box" that magically confers social-emotional competencies, and arts educators who treat it as such are missing the chance to leverage the learning opportunities that the arts provide.

Instead, we argue that the real power of arts education to affect social-emotional outcomes lies in the moments of art practice and the corresponding social-emotional components of these practices. By paying attention to these components, arts educators can fully leverage the opportunities to promote social-emotional learning.

We heard from many students, parents, and teachers about arts education experiences that contributed in important ways to students' social and emotional growth. We heard about how students' confidence grew when they realized they had created something special in a visual arts context, about students who persisted through a challenging learning process in a dance class, and about students who better understood their own and others' emotions when participating in a theatre program.

But there was also plenty we didn't hear. Not every student takes the same social and emotional lesson away from a given visual art, dance, or theatre experience. Some students' visual arts creations don't breed confidence in their creative abilities; some dance students don't persist; and some theatre students are unable to tap into the emotions of the characters they're playing. Indeed, for some students, these experiences can leave more of a negative imprint than a positive one. Moreover, even among students who do take something positive away from an arts education experience, this research has made clear that there is not a tight fit between specific arts disciplines and the social and emotional growth opportunities they can afford. How an instructor teaches often matters more than what they teach.

This is exactly why intentionality in leveraging the opportunities afforded by arts education is so critical. In the hands of a skilled arts educator who pays close attention to how students are engaging socially and emotionally in the developmental experience of the art practices they're bringing to their students, even these more negative or upsetting experiences can lead to growth. This does not mean that being intentional about leveraging social-emotional components is easy. To the contrary, doing intentional social-emotional work can be quite difficult at times and is not necessarily a skill that is taught in teacher-training programs. Some might even argue that supporting students' social-emotional development is instinctual—that it comes naturally to some instructors but less so to others.

At the same time, the ideas presented here should not be foreign to most educators. Many existing instructional frameworks emphasize the important role teachers play in creating an environment that is psychologically safe and engaging for learners, and for providing opportunities for students to practice self-management, build strong interpersonal and relationship skills, and engage in healthy self-expression. The definition of distinguished teaching in the Classroom Environment domain in the Chicago Public Schools' *Framework for Teaching,* for example, includes language like, "students initiate respectful interactions with peers and teacher," and "students take an active role in promoting respect and showing care about individual classmates' interests and personalities."[77] Where social-emotional learning standards exist,[78] aligning these standards with arts learning standards is another strategy for being intentional about taking advantage of the social-emotional affordances that might be available in a curriculum and its associated art practices. In calling for educators to be intentional in their efforts to promote social and emotional growth integrated within their academic discipline, this project builds on and is consistent with findings in the growing literature on social-emotional learning.[79] To provide opportunities for children and adolescents to develop in a holistic manner, it is important to provide scaffolding for social-emotional learning concepts, just as is the case when teaching math or other academic content.[80] Supporting students' social-emotional development encompasses a range of instructional approaches that must be implemented intentionally; students should have opportunities to explicitly learn about and apply social and emotional skills throughout their school day and in their after-school settings.[81] Relatedly, *Foundations for Young Adult Success: A Developmental Framework* discusses the important role trusted adults can play in fostering opportunities for social and emotional growth—both by building supportive developmental relationships with and crafting developmental experiences for their students. Developmental experiences offer opportunities for young people to engage in various forms of action and reflection. It is through ongoing cycles of age-appropriate action and reflection experiences that young people build the four foundational components of long-term success (self-regulation, knowledge and skills, mindsets, and values) and develop agency, an integrated identity, and socially valued competencies.[82]

Lessons for Other Subjects

Students and parents in this research tended to value the arts in large part because of the opportunities they presented for social and emotional growth, and because of how different their arts experiences were than their experiences in their conventional academic classrooms. From the idea that arts education should be conducted in "safe spaces" to the frequent focus on identity, movement, and self-discovery, arts educators frequently employ creative pedagogical strategies intended to engage students, and parents notice and value these strategies.

These differences between arts education and other educational contexts may not need to be as pronounced as they seem to be in most places today. Developmental experiences are at the core of social-emotional development, and there is nothing magical about the arts when it comes to providing opportunities for young people to engage in action (encountering, tinkering, choosing, practicing, and contributing) or reflection (describing, evaluating, connecting, envisioning, and integrating) experiences. Educators at large could explore ways to translate some arts educators' strategies to their own classrooms, and could approach this translation creatively and without rigid preconceptions about which strategies can or cannot work for a given academic field or discipline.

For example, there does not appear to be anything inherent in or distinctive about the arts that makes it *more* essential for arts educators (as compared to educators in other subject areas) to create emotionally safe spaces for learning. The idea that learning and social and emotional growth are best facilitated when the classroom is a safe space—when students experience a sense of belonging and feel like they can trust the others in the room—is being more widely recognized in education contexts outside the arts.[83] While arts teachers by no means have a monopoly on the right strategies for achieving this kind of safe environment, the fact that this is such a common theme in arts education suggests that educators at large can and should draw inspiration

---

77 See also the Arts Addendum to the CPS Framework for Teaching (http://www.cpsarts.org/artsaddendum/) and, for teaching artists, the Arts Partner Standards of Practice (https://www.ingenuity-inc.org/quality-initiative).
78 For example, see Illinois' Social Emotional Learning Standards (https://www.isbe.net/pages/social-emotional-learning-standards.aspx).
79 See also the Positive Youth Development literature (e.g., Development Services Group, Inc., 2015; Durlak et al., 2007; Heck & Subramaniam, 2009).
80 The Aspen Institute (2017).
81 Jones & Kahn (2017).
82 Nagaoka et al. (2015).
83 Allensworth et al. (2018); Berman, Chaffee, & Sarmiento (2018); Farrington et al. (2012).

from the pedagogical and relational strategies used by arts educators.

Beyond creating safe spaces, educators outside the arts may be able to leverage some of the other opportunities that currently tend to be concentrated in the arts. Who is to say that science or math could not be taught in highly differentiated, relationship-driven ways that recognize the social aspects of teamwork or the emotional aspects of public performance? What can other educators learn from the connections that some arts students have with their arts educators? How can the freedom to move around in many arts education classrooms, and the benefits this freedom provides, be brought to other classrooms? The distinctiveness of arts classrooms may reflect generalizable pedagogical practices that could be used more often in other educational contexts (e.g., math or science classes), and educators in these other contexts could utilize these practices to more effectively achieve both academic and social-emotional learning goals.[84] Arts integration into traditional academic classrooms may also help educators in traditional fields envision and experiment with new possibilities.

What Research Is Needed

Historically, education research too often has approached evaluating the effects of education from a deficit perspective. This also applies to much of the research on the effects of arts education reviewed for this report. In other words, research questions are often framed as whether "arts exposure" or participation in a formal arts program has positive effects on an "at-risk" or stigmatized group that reduces "gaps" between them and their more advantaged peers. This line of inquiry has led to a narrowing of how researchers describe the myriad ways that young people engage with artistic and creative practices, particularly those outside of culturally sanctioned artistic venues. The arts education research base could benefit from a more expansive view of what arts are and how students' backgrounds and identity come into play in their engagement with the arts.

Perhaps the greatest need is for applied research that better articulates and explores the ways that specific art practices and pedagogical strategies in different contexts lead to different social-emotional competencies. Rather than asking "Does this arts program result in X outcomes?" researchers instead might ask "What are the mechanisms whereby particular arts activities support the development of specific social-emotional competencies?" While we would not argue in favor of an attempt to build a "recipe" for social-emotional learning through the arts, we do believe there is great potential value in being able to provide more research-based tools for arts educators who want to be intentional about their pedagogical approaches to social-emotional development. Important research questions for future studies might include: What opportunities do particular art practices provide for social-emotional development? Do the social-emotional affordances of a particular art practice vary, depending on the art form? How does a student's interest in an art form affect the social-emotional outcomes of participation? How might arts educators intentionally draw on students' cultural or other assets to increase the developmental effectiveness of particular art practices? How does the context in which an arts education process takes place affect the social-emotional outcomes of participation?

This project also highlights the need for a deeper understanding of the transferability of social-emotional components and how scaffolding of social-emotional learning outcomes happens. While our focus here has been on arts education, social-emotional learning opportunities emerge throughout students' lives, and we know little about where and how the social and emotional lessons learned in one context transfer to other contexts, or how they may build upon one another. There are also relatively few mechanisms for coordinating efforts among the different adult actors that are connected to students' lives.

Conclusion

The role that arts education plays in the school day has evolved over time, from being a subject with intrinsic value as a part of a well-rounded education, to being an instrument to improve school engagement and academic performance, to being a means of fostering social-emotional development. The potential value of arts education lies at the crossroads of these roles. It is also shaped by a widely shared cultural understanding of art as being a way to express emotions and ideas to others, as well as the emerging research consensus about the deep interconnections among cognitive, emotional, and social-relational aspects of human functioning. Arts education has often been placed at the periphery of the education world. But as our understanding about the process of learning improves, and as evidence mounts that learning is a deeply, fundamentally social and

---

84 Many instructional frameworks (e.g., the CPS Framework for Teaching) already embed some of these concepts in their definitions of quality teaching practices, and in most cases these definitions are intended to apply to all content areas.

emotional as well as cultural process, it becomes clearer how and why arts education has much to contribute to children's education and how, in the end, it can help schools and other institutions better support young people in becoming emotionally healthy, engaged, and productive adults.

Hyde Park Art Center

WORKS CITED

Alemán, X., Duryea, S., Guerra, N. G., McEwan, P. J., Muñoz, R., Stampini, M., & Williamson, A. A. (2016). The effects of musical training on child development: A randomized trial of *El Sistema* in Venezuela. *Prevention Science, 17*, 1-14.

Allensworth, E. M., Farrington, C. A., Gordon, M. F., Johnson, D. W., Klein, K., McDaniel, B., & Nagaoka, J. (2018). *Supporting social, emotional, & academic development: Research implications for educators.* Chicago, IL: University of Chicago Consortium on School Research.

Asbury, C., & Rich, B. (Eds.). (2008). *Learning, arts, and the brain: The Dana Consortium report on arts and cognition.* New York, NY: Dana Press.

Aspen Institute. (2017). *How learning happens: Supporting students' social, emotional, and academic development.* Washington, DC: The Aspen Institute.

Baker, S., & Homan, S. (2007). Rap, recidivism and the creative self: A popular music program for young offenders in detention. *Journal of Youth Studies, 10*(4), 459-476.

Barrett, M. S., & Bond, N. (2014). Connecting through music: The contribution of a music programme to fostering positive youth development. *Research Studies in Music Education, 37*(1), 37-54.

Bartel, L. R., & Cameron, L. M. (2002, April 3). *Pedagogical dilemmas in dance and music: Balancing the demands of the art with the needs of the person.* Paper presented at the American Education Research Association Annual Conference, New Orleans, LA.

Beales, J. N., & Zemel, B. (1990). The effects of high school drama on social maturity. *The School Counselor, 38*(1), 46-51.

Becker, H. S. (2008). *Art worlds: 25th anniversary edition, updated and expanded* (1st Ed.). Los Angeles, CA: University of California Press.

Bergmann, S. (1995). Creative dance in the education curriculum: Justifying the unambiguous. *Canadian Journal of Education, 20*(2), 156-165.

Berman, S., Chaffee, S., & Sarmiento, J. (2018). *The practice base for how we learn: Supporting students' social, emotional, and academic development.* Washington, DC: National Commission on Social, Emotional, and Academic Development.

Best, D. (1978). Emotional education through the arts. *The Journal of Aesthetic Education, 12*(2), 71-84.

Blatner, A. (1995). Drama in education as mental hygiene: A child psychiatrist's perspective. *Youth Theatre Journal, 9*(1), 92-96.

Borba, M. (2018). *Nine competencies for teaching empathy. Educational Leadership, 76*(2), 22-28.

Brinda, W. (2008). Building literacy bridges for adolescents using Holocaust literature and theatre. *The Journal of Aesthetic Education, 42*(4), 31-44.

Brouillette, L., Irvine, Childress-Evans, K., Hinga, B., Irvine, & Farkas, G. (2014). Increasing the school engagement and oral language skills of ELLs through arts integration in the primary grades. *Journal for Learning through the Arts, 10*(1), 1-25.

Brown, E. D., & Sax, K. L. (2013). Arts enrichment and preschool emotions for low-income children at risk. *Early Childhood Research Quarterly, 28*(1), 337-346.

Burnaford, G., Brown, S., Doherty, J., & McLaughlin, H. J. (2007). *Arts integration frameworks, research, and practice: A literature review.* Denver, CO: Arts Education Partnership.

Campbell, L. H. (2006). Spirituality and holistic art education. *Visual Arts Research, 32*(1), 29-34.

Cantor, P., Osher, D., Berg, J., Steyer, L., & Rose, T. (2018). Malleability, plasticity, and individuality: How children learn and develop in context. *Applied Developmental Science.* doi:10.1080/10888691.2017.1398649

Catterall, J. S., Dumais, S. A., & Hampden-Thompson, G. (2012). *The arts and achievement in at-risk youth: Findings from four longitudinal studies.* Washington, DC: National Endowment for the Arts.

Catterall, J. S., & Peppler, K. A. (2007). Learning in the visual arts and the worldviews of young children. *Cambridge Journal of Education, 37*(4), 543-560.

College Board. (2012). Child development and arts education: A review of current research and best practices. New York, NY: The College Board.

Collins, R., & Cooper, P. A. (1997). *The power of story: Teaching through storytelling* (2nd Ed.). Needham Heights, MA: Allyn & Bacon.

Davis, V. W. (2009). The meaning of music education to middle school general music students. *Bulletin of the Council for Research in Music Education, 179,* 61-77.

Deasy, R. J. (Ed.) (2002). *Critical links: Learning in the arts and student academic and social development.* Washington, DC: Arts Education Partnership.

Dee, T. S. (2005). A teacher like me. Does race, ethnicity, or gender matter? *The American Economic Review, 95*(2), 158-165.

Development Services Group, I. (2015). Literature review: Positive youth development. In Rockville, MD: National Registry of Evidence-based Programs and Practices.

Dewey, J. (1954). *Art as experience.* New York, NY: Penguin Group.

Dow, C. B. (2010). Young children and movement: The power of creative dance. *YC Young Children, 65*(2), 30-35.

Durlak, J. A., Taylor, R. D., Kawashima, K., Pachan, M. K., DuPre, E. P., Celio, C. I., . . . Weissberg, R. P. (2007). Effects of positive youth development programs on school, family, and community systems. *American Journal of Community Psychology, 39*(3/4), 269-286.

Eccles, J., & Gootman, J. A. (2002). *Community programs to promote youth development.* Washington, DC: National Academy Press.

Egalite, A. J., Kisida, B., & Winters, M. A. (2015). Representation in the classroom: The effect of own-race teachers on student achievement. *Economics of Education Review, 45,* 44-52.

Farnum, M., & Schaffer, R. (1998). YouthARTS handbook: Art programs for youth at risk. In Washington, DC: Americans for the Arts.

Farrington, C. A., Porter, S., & Klugman, J. (forthcoming). *Do classroom environments matter for noncognitive aspects of student performance and students' course grades?* Chicago, IL: University of Chicago Consortium on School Research.

Farrington, C. A., Roderick, M., Allensworth, E., Nagaoka, J., Keyes, T. S., Johnson, D. W., & Beechum, N. O. (2012). *Teaching adolescents to become learners: The role of noncognitive factors in shaping school performance: A critical literature review.* Chicago, IL: University of Chicago Consortium on Chicago School Research.

Fiske, E. B. (Ed.) (1999). *Champions of change: The impact of the arts on learning*. Washington, DC: The Arts Education Partnership.

Foster, E. M., & Marcus Jenkins, J. V. (2017). Does participation in music and performing arts influence child development? *American Educational Research Journal, 54*(3), 399-443.

Freeman, G. D., Sullivan, K., & Fulton, C. R. (2003). Effects of creative drama on self-concept, social skills, and problem behavior. *The Journal of Educational Research, 96*(3), 131-138.

Gallagher, K., Ntelioglou, B. Y., & Wessels, A. (2013). "Listening to the affective life of injustice": Drama pedagogy, race, identity, and learning. *Youth Theatre Journal, 27*(1), 7-19.

Gaztambide-Fernandez, R. A. (2013). Why the arts don't do anything: Toward a new vision for cultural production in education. *Harvard Educational Review, 83*(1), 211-236.

Goffman, E. (1974). *Frame analysis: An essay on the organization of experience*. Cambridge, MA: Harvard University Press.

Green, J., & Kindseth, A. (2011). Art all day: Distinction and interrelation of school-based and out-of-school arts learning. *Studies in Art Education, 52*(4), 337-341.

Gullatt, D. E. (2008). Enhancing student learning through arts integration: Implications for the profession. *The High School Journal, 91*(4), 12-25.

Hanna, J. L. (2008). A nonverbal language for imagining and learning: Dance education in K-12 curriculum. *Educational Researcher, 37*(8), 491-506.

Hardiman, M. M. (2016). Education and the arts: Educating every child in the spirit of inquiry and joy. *Creative Education, 7*, 1913-1928.

Harman, R., & Smagorinsky, P. (2014). A critical performative process: Supporting the second-language literacies and voices of emergent bilingual learners. *Youth Theatre Journal, 28*(2), 147-164.

Heck, K. E., & Subramaniam, A. (2009). *Youth development frameworks [Monograph]*. Davis, CA: 4-H Center for Youth Development, University of California.

Hetland, L., & Winner, E. (2001). The arts and academic achievement: What the evidence shows. *Arts Education Policy Review, 102*(5), 3-6.

Hetland, L., & Winner, E. (2004). Cognitive transfer from arts education to non-arts outcomes: Research evidence and policy implications. In E. Eisner & M. Day (Eds.), *Handbook on research and policy in arts education*, 135-161. Washington, DC: National Art Education Association.

Holochwost, S. J., Wolf, D. P., Fisher, K. R., & O'Grady, K. (2017). *The socioemotional benefits of the arts: A new mandate for arts education*. Philadelphia, PA: William Penn Foundation.

Hoxie, A. M. E., & Debellis, L. M. (2014). Engagement in out-of-school time: How youth become engaged in the arts. *National Society for the Study of Education, 113*(1), 219-231.

Hylton, J. B. (1981). Dimensionality in high school student participants' perceptions of the meaning of choral singing experience. *Journal of Research in Music Education, 29*(4), 287-303.

Immordino-Yang, M. H. (2016). *Emotions, learning, and the brain: Exploring the educational implications of affective neuroscience*. New York, NY: W. W. Norton & Co.

Jones, S. M., & Kahn, J. (2017). *The evidence base for how we learn: Supporting students' social, emotional, and academic development. Consensus statements of evidence from the Council of Distinguished Scientists*. Washington, DC: The Aspen Institute.

Kahn, B. B. (1999). Art therapy with adolescents: Making it work for school counselors. *American School Counselor Association, 2*(4), 291-298.

Katz, M. L. (2008). Growth in motion: Supporting young women's embodied identity and cognitive development through dance after school. *Afterschool Matters, 7*, 12-22.

Kisiel, C., Blaustein, M., Spinazzola, J., Schmidt, C. S., Zucker, M., & van der Kolk, B. (2006). Evaluation of a theatre-based youth violence prevention program for elementary school children. *Journal of School Violence, 5*(2), 19-36.

Knowles, P. (1993). Dance education in American public schools. *Bulletin of the Council for Research in Music Education, 117,* 46-50.

Kudo, I., & Hartley, J. (2017, August 25). Teaching (with) empathy and compassion in schools. *Education for Global Development Blog.* Retrieved from http://blogs.worldbank.org/education/teaching-empathy-and-compassion-schools

Kuhl, P. K. (2004). Early language acquisition: Cracking the speech code. *Nature Reviews Neuroscience, 5*(11), 831-843.

Ladson-Billings, G. (1994). *The dreamkeepers: Successful teachers of African American children* (1st Ed.). San Francisco, CA: Jossey-Bass Publishing Co.

Larson, R. W., & Brown, J. R. (2007). Emotional development in adolescence: What can be learned from a high school theater program? *Child Development, 78*(4), 1083-1099.

Lerner, M. D., & Mikami, A. Y. (2012). A preliminary randomized controlled trial of two social skills interventions for youth with high-functioning autism spectrum disorders. *Focus on Autism and Other Developmental Disabilities, 27*(3), 147-157.

Ludwig, M., Marklein, M. B., & Song, M. (2016). *Arts integration: A promising approach to improving early learning.* Washington, DC: American Institutes for Research.

Macy, L. (2004). A novel study through drama. *The Reading Teacher, 58*(3), 240-248.

Mages, W. K. (2010). Creating a culture of collaboration: The conception, design, and evolution of a Head Start theatre-in-education program. *Youth Theatre Journal, 24*(1), 45-61.

McBride, M. R. A., & Maurer, J. (2016). *Quality initiative: Phase one report.* Chicago, IL: Ingenuity.

McCammon, L. A., Saldaña, J., Hines, A., & Omasta, M. (2012). Lifelong impact: Adult perceptions of their high school speech and/or theatre participation. *Youth Theatre Journal, 26*(1), 2-25.

Melnick, S. A., Witmer, J. T., & Strickland, M. J. (2008). *Cognition and student learning through the arts.* Paper presented at the Northeastern Educational Research Association Annual Conference, Trumbull, CT.

Miksza, P. (2013). The future of music education: Continuing the dialogue about curricular reform. *Music Educators Journal, 99*(4), 45-50.

Nagaoka, J., Farrington, C. A., Ehrlich, S. B., Heath, R. D., Johnson, D. W., Dickson, S., . . . Hayes, K. (2015). *Foundations for young adult success: A developmental framework.* Chicago, IL: University of Chicago Consortium on Chicago School Research.

National Research Council. (2012). *Education for life and work: Developing transferable knowledge and skills in the 21st century.* Washington, DC: The National Academies Press.

Pellegrini, A. D., & Galda, L. (1982). The effects of thematic-fantasy play training on the development of children's story comprehension. *American Educational Research Journal, 19*(3), 443-452.

Pulido, I. (2009). "Music fit for us minorities:" Latinas/os' use of hip hop as pedagogy and interpretive framework to negotiate and challenge racism. *Equity & Excellence in Education, 42*(1), 67-85.

Richards, E. W. (2011). Social and musical objectives or experiences school music teachers anticipate their students will achieve as a result of attending a summer music camp. *Contributions to Music Education, 38*(2), 61-72.

Richardson, K. (2017). Genes, brains, and human potential: *The science and ideology of intelligence.* New York, NY: Columbia University Press.

Rivkin, J. (2009). *The empathic civilization: The race to global consciousness in a world in crisis.* New York, NY: Penguin.

Rodríguez, L. F. (2009). Dialoguing, cultural capital, and student engagement: Toward a hip hop pedagogy in the high school and university classroom. *Equity & Excellence in Education, 42*(1), 20-15.

Rose, D. S., Parks, M., Androes, K., & McMahon, S. D. (2000). Imagery-based learning: Improving elementary students' reading comprehension with drama techniques. *The Journal of Educational Research, 94*(1), 55-63.

Runfola, M., Etopio, E., Hamlen, K., & Rozendal, M. (2012). Effect of music instruction on preschoolers' music achievement and emergent literacy achievement. *Bulletin of the Council for Research in Music Education, 192*, 7-27.

Ruppert, S. S. (2006). *Critical evidence: How the ARTS benefit student achievement*. Washington, DC: National Assembly of State Arts Agencies.

Rusk, N., Larson, R. W., Raffaelli, M., Walker, K., Washington, L., Gutierrez, V., . . . Perry, S. C. (2013). Positive youth development in organized programs: How teens learn to manage emotions. In C. Proctor & P. A. Linley (Ed.), *Research, applications, and interventions for children and adolescents: A positive psychology perspective*. Dordrecht, Netherlands: Springer Science+Business Media Dordrecht.

Sansom, A. N. (2011). The development of dance education in New Zealand. *Counterpoints, 407*, 11-24.

Scripp, L. (2007). *A final report: Developing early literacies through the arts*. Chicago, IL: Chicago Arts Partnerships in Education.

Search Institute. (2014). *A research update from Search Institute: Developmental relationships*. Minneapolis, MN: The Search Institute.

Spencer-Keyse, J. (2018, March 6). Educating empathy: Inspiring students to develop their passions. *Education Plus Development Blog*. Retrieved from https://www.brookings.edu/blog/education-plus-development/2018/03/06/educating-empathy-inspiring-students-to-develop-their-passions/

Taliaferro Baszile, D. (2009). Deal with it we must: Education, social justice, and the curriculum of hip hop culture. *Equity & Excellence in Education, 42*(1), 6-19.

Ulfarsdottir, L. O., & Erwin, P. G. (1999). The influence of music on social cognitive skills. *The Arts in Psychotherapy, 26*(2), 81-84.

Walker, E., Tabone, C., & Weltsek, G. (2011). When achievement data meet drama and arts integration. *Language Arts, 88*(5), 365-372.

Walker, E. M., McFadden, L. B., Tabone, C., & Finkelstein, M. (2011). Contribution of drama-based strategies. *Youth Theatre Journal, 25*(1), 3-15.

Walsh-Bowers, R., & Basso, R. (1999). Improving early adolescents' peer relations through classroom creative drama: An integrated approach. *Social Work in Education, 21*(1), 23-32.

Walton, G. M., & Cohen, G. L. (2007). A question of belonging: Race, social fit, and achievement. *Journal of Personality and Social Psychology, 92*(1), 82-96.

Walton, G. M., & Cohen, G. L. (2011). A brief social-belonging intervention improves academic and health outcomes among minority students. *Science, 331*(6023), 1447-1451.

Wright, R., John, L., Alaggia, R., & Sheel, J. (2006). Community-based arts program for youth in low-income communities: A multi-method evaluation. *Child and Adolescent Social Work Journal, 23*(5-6), 635-652.

Zimmerman, E. (2009). Reconceptualizing the role of creativity in art education theory and practice. *Studies in Art Education, 50*(4), 382-399.

Zimmerman, E., & Zimmerman, L. (2000). Art education and early childhood education: The young child as creator and meaning maker within a community context. *Young Children, 55*(6), 87-92.

ACKNOWLEDGMENTS

The authors gratefully acknowledge the members of the project Steering Committee for their feedback and guidance.

Jane Best | Executive Director, Arts Education Partnership

Kim Cassel | Director of Evidence-Based Policy, Arnold Ventures

Adele Diamond | Professor, Developmental Cognitive Neuroscience, Department of Psychiatry, University of British Columbia

Aaron Dworkin | Professor of Arts Leadership & Entrepreneurship, University of Michigan School of Music, Theatre, & Dance

Paul Goren | Superintendent, District 65 Schools

Reed Larson | Professor Emeritus, Human Development and Family Studies, University of Illinois, Urbana-Champaign

Bronwyn Nichols Lodato | Fellow, The Committee on Education at The University of Chicago

Jorge Lucero | Associate Professor & Chair of Art Education, School of Art + Design, University of Illinois, Urbana-Champaign

LaTanya McDade | Chief Education Officer, Chicago Public Schools

Ashlyn Aiko Nelson | Associate Professor of Economics, Indiana University School of Public and Environmental Affairs

James Pellegrino | Distinguished Professor of Liberal Arts and Sciences, Psychology and Education, University of Illinois at Chicago

Evan Plummer | Former Director of Arts Education, Chicago Public Schools

Sydney Sidwell | Director of Education and Arts Learning, Lloyd A. Fry Foundation

Paul Sznewajs | Executive Director, Ingenuity

We especially thank Sydney Sidwell for her thought partnership throughout the process. We also thank the members of the UChicago Consortium's research review group, particularly Bronwyn McDaniel and Nicole Beechum, who provided valuable feedback. We are grateful to the members of the UChicago Consortium Steering Committee—especially, Raquel Farmer-Hinton—who served as readers for the penultimate draft. We further thank Rosa Gonzalez for assisting throughout the process. Finally, the communications teams at Ingenuity, UChicago Consortium, and UChicago UEI—Karla Rivera, Jessica Tansey, Jessica Puller, Alida Mitau, and Dayna Dion—were instrumental in the production of this report.

We would also like to thank all of the students and their families, arts educators, teaching artists, and arts education leaders who took the time to speak with us about their experiences and helped shape our thinking and the content of this report.

The research reported in this report was made possible by a grant from the Spencer Foundation (#201700060). The views expressed are those of the authors and do not necessarily reflect the views of the Spencer Foundation. We are particularly grateful to John Easton and Michael Barber, our program officers at the Spencer Foundation, for conceptualizing and supporting this project throughout its development.

The UChicago Consortium greatly appreciates support from the Consortium Investor Council that funds critical work beyond the initial research: putting the research to work, refreshing the data archive, seeding new studies, and replicating previous studies. Members include: Brinson Foundation, Chicago Community Trust, CME Group Foundation, The Crown Family, Joyce Foundation, Lewis-Sebring Family Foundation, Lloyd A. Fry Foundation, McDougal Family Foundation, Robert R. McCormick Foundation, Osa Foundation, Polk Bros. Foundation, Spencer Foundation, Steans Family Foundation, Square One Foundation, and the Chicago Public Education Fund.

The UChicago Consortium is also grateful for the operating grants from the Spencer Foundation and the Lewis-Sebring Family Foundation that support the work of the UChicago Consortium.